Understanding
Green Building Materials

Understanding
Green Building Materials

**Traci Rose Rider,
Stacy Glass, &
Jessica McNaughton**

Edited by Karen Levine

W. W. Norton & Company
New York • London

For information about permission to reproduce selections from this book,
write to Permissions, W. W. Norton & Company, Inc., 500 Fifth Avenue,
New York, NY 10110

For information about special discounts for bulk purchases, please contact
W. W. Norton Special Sales at secialsales@wwnorton.com or 800-233-4830.

Book design by Jonathan Lippincott
Composition by Ken Gross
Manufacturing by Courier Westford
Production Manager: Leeann Graham

Library of Congress Cataloging-in-Publication Data

Rider, Traci Rose.
    Understanding green building materials / Traci Rose Rider, Stacy Glass, Jessica
McNaughton.
        p.   cm.
    Includes bibliographical references and index.
    ISBN 978-0-393-73317-4 (pbk.)
    1. Building materials—Environmental aspects. 2. Green products. I. Glass, Stacy
(Stacy N.), 1970– II. McNaughton, Jessica. III. Title.

TD196.B85R53   2011
721'.046—dc22   2010031301

W. W. Norton & Company, Inc.,
500 Fifth Avenue, New York, N.Y. 10110
www.wwnorton.com

W. W. Norton & Company Ltd.,
Castle House, 75/76 Wells St., London W1T 3QT

0 9 8 7 6 5 4 3 2 1

This book was printed on 80# Utopia Book, which is FSC-certified. The Forest
Stewardship Council (FSC) sets forth principles, criteria, and standards for the
wood fiber industry that span economic, social, and environmental concerns,
meaning that the paper has passed through a complete "chain of custody" from
an FSC-certified forest, to an FSC-certified paper manufacturer, to an FSC-certified merchant, and an FSC-certified printer. Each part of the chain has its own
standards for compliance. The paper contains 10 percent post-consumer waste,
and is elemental-chlorine free.

According to the paper mill's Web site (appletoncoated.com), use of this paper
yields

Trees Saved: 3
    Post-consumer recovered fiber (PCRF) displaces wood fiber with savings trans-
    lated as trees. (The number of typical trees assumes a mix of hardwoods and
    softwoods 6–8" in diameter and 40' tall.)

Energy Saved: 2.2 million BTUs
    PCRF content displaces energy used to process equivalent virgin fiber. (The
    average U.S. household uses 91 million BTUs of energy in a year.)

First, to anyone with the energy and passion for a greener world, convinced they can make a difference. The best is yet to come and you can absolutely be a part of it! And second, to my little brother and all soldiers serving in Afghanistan—stay safe!

—*Traci Rose Rider*

This book is dedicated to the next generation of architects and designers, who will bring these relatively new ideas to life and make "green" and sustainable principles part of our everyday built environment.

—*Stacy Glass*

To all the people who started thinking "green" long before the rest of us, and had the foresight to get us to where we are today; and to all those who will keep pushing, innovating, and bringing to market the products and ideas that will propel the initiative further.

Jessica McNaughton

Contents

Acknowledgments

I am lucky that encouragement, patience, and optimism abound in my life. Thank you to all my friends and colleagues; you inspire me daily. A special thank you to Susannah Tuttle, who is always helping me find a path. Thanks to my mom and dad, who are incredible in both their methods and their amount of support and belief. A huge thanks to my husband, Dan, for humoring me in all my disparate and time-consuming projects. You are very good to me. And a special thanks to my favorite little guy, Beckett, for allowing me to write and edit in spurts between playing, wrestling, running, drumming, and enjoying a wonderfully happy two-year-old.

— *Traci Rose Rider*

Thank you to the team who founded CaraGreen as a passionate pursuit of beautiful, innovative, and sustainable building material. I also want to express my appreciation to the CaraGreen team, and their daily commitment to being an educational resource for accurate information on sustainable materials. Finally, I want to thank my husband, Jeff Glass, for his support and patience during this entrepreneurial endeavor.

— *Stacy Glass*

I would like to thank CaraGreen for its support while writing this book and for the extensive network of partners that helped to contribute to our efforts to put together a comprehensive look at sustainable building materials. Also, much thanks to my husband, Sean, who patiently endured months of drafting and editing, and to our son Sebastian, who waited to arrive until the book was submitted for editing. I love you both very much.

— *Jessica McNaughton*

Understanding
Green Building Materials

Introduction: What Is Green Design?

In today's world, "green" seems to be everywhere, in every-thing, and on everyone's lips. There is no denying that the green building movement has made giant strides in the first decade of the twenty-first century. Energy-efficient design popular in the 1970s shifted to the fringe as energy issues slid by the wayside in the 1980s. Today, however, energy-efficient design is back— abundantly so—but with a sleek new look that is sophisticated and no longer subservient to the older stereo-typical forms, aesthetics, or outdated energy reduction strate-gies. Today, pairing energy efficiency with other issues (such as occupant health and resource conservation) has become the focus of current green design strategies and construction methodologies.

Recognizing that the green building movement has per-meated the building industry and become the standard is the easy part. The hard part is to understand what "green" design really is. Beyond the vague and hard-to-define terms surround-ing the movement—green, sustainable, regenerative, healthy,

energy-efficient, carbon-neutral, zero-energy, etc.—there are endless nuances you'll have to wrap your head around as you dig deeper into each sub-category of the field. What are the actual components that create a "green" project? What thresh-olds must you cross to achieve "green" status? What bound-aries and criteria must you pay attention to at the scale of the building, the site, the community, the region? Which of these must be dealt with during the design process? And, equally important, what do you *not* need to worry about?

How do designers and project teams begin to address these issues without imploding? One step at a time—and that's what this book is designed to do.

Broad in scope, the realm of green design embraces many facets not traditionally incorporated in the design and build-ing process. For many, the criteria promulgated in the early days of the green movement seemed vague and ever-chang-ing, a criticism that was to some extent legitimate as the move-ment strove to find its way, articulating, testing, and refining appropriate criteria. In response to the concerns about clarity, groups began to break the green realm down into more manageable pieces. Organizations such as the U.S. Green Building Council (USGBC) and the Green Building Initiative (GBI) were formed, creating building rating systems and guidelines to group important considerations into distinct categories. Other entities—which were more mature and had been addressing discrete elements of green design for years, such as the American Society of Heating, Refrigerating, and Air-Conditioning Engineers (ASHRAE)—were brought closer into the green building fold to contribute their knowledge and expertise. Still other organizations were created or strengthened to fill a demand and help establish metrics and verification for specific materials and processes.

Today, thanks to the efforts of these organizations and the standards they've created, we have the essential categories and criteria to design and build green projects. True, the energy efficiency highlighted in the 1970s remains a driving force behind green building, providing immediate, quantitative results documented by the cost savings associated with the reduced energy usage. Yet energy efficiency is not the only goal for creating green buildings; nor are sealing the building envelope and making the use of solar panels unconditionally acceptable or the sole criteria for green buildings. Other factors such as water usage, air quality, the amount and quality of lighting, and the location of both the property and the building are now considerations that also require attention.

By compartmentalizing in this way, proponents of green building have created functional categories at the project level. These categories enable designers and contractors to incorporate sustainable features and functions according to a specific set of criteria for each category. In addition to energy, water, and occupant health, material selection and resource use have become integral considerations in the creation of green buildings.

Our goal in writing this book is to create a framework for material selection that will empower you to ask manufacturers pertinent questions about their products as well as advise you regarding the product attributes that should receive careful thought during your selection process. Basic considerations are explored, common concerns noted, and consistent threads identified. We've focused primarily, although not exclusively, on interior materials. You'll find that you can generalize the foundation of material knowledge we present to evaluate material selections beyond those addressed in this book.

Another important aspect of material evaluation is the overarching concept of life cycle assessment (LCA). Explained in more detail in Chapter 4, LCA is the investigation and evaluation of the environmental impacts of a given product (or service). This concept is so broad that reining in the many considerations to a manageable set of metrics has proven to be incredibly difficult. Many options and proposals on how to perform LCA are under consideration; however, when this book went to press, no single assessment tool for this process was yet agreed upon. Nevertheless, we discuss what comprises LCA and why it is a valuable tool in helping you to make sustainable choices in any material category.

The current alternative to a complete life cycle assessment is a careful consideration of the sustainable features that can and should be evaluated for each material to be used in a project. To simplify the process, we have broken down material selection into these recognized industry-defined categories:

- Structural Materials (concrete, brick, steel, etc.)
- Wall Systems (insulation, framing lumber, sheetrock, SIPS panels, etc.)
- Floor Systems (carpets, hardwood, cork, linoleum, bamboo, tile, etc.)
- Countertops
- Millwork
- Furniture (fabric, framing)
- Finishes (primers, paints, sealants, adhesives, and coatings)

For each material, we discuss the following: composition of the standard material; concerns and objections associated with that material (i.e., embodied energy and toxicity); green alternatives to the standard selections; and trends in the evolution of these alternatives. We outline issues and innovations related to the building materials covered and, because our goal throughout is to help you understand what to look for and what to avoid, we also examine various labels and certification programs that have emerged to help identify good and bad attributes of products.

So, before we launch into the exploration of the materials themselves, category by category, let's begin by taking a look at the most common rating systems and material-related credits widely used in green building today. In the process, we'll explore where overlaps exist between the systems and among the specific credits, and highlight what factors are most relevant in each rating system.

Chapter 1: Green Building Rating Systems

If you're searching for green materials, you probably already know that it takes more than a product's marketing claims to qualify it as a sustainable material. A number of whole building rating systems address green materials within their scope, the most common being the U.S. Green Building Council's (USGBC) Leadership in Energy and Environmental Design (LEED), the Green Building Initiative's (GBI) Green Globes, and the National Association of Home Builders' (NAHB) National Green Building Standard, which focuses primarily on residential construction. You may be familiar with one or more of these national systems, or with any number of local green building guidelines. Suffice it to say, they all address material choice in one way or another, so it is helpful to take a look at how materials are viewed within these prevalent rating systems as well as how the systems may differ.

It's worth noting that while similar issues are addressed in the various rating systems, the way in which they are addressed hinges on the structure and layout of the individual rating system and its particular guidelines. For example, while the LEED system and the NAHB Standard tend to be prescriptive methods, focusing on the end result and strategies that are employed in a certified building, the Green Globes system walks the design team through each step of the process, prodding for decisions and encouraging different levels of consideration throughout the project timeline.

Both the LEED system and the NAHB Standard rely on a single, comprehensive checklist. LEED can be completed and submitted for review in two stages: at the end of design (after construction documents are issued) and after completion of construction. The option also exists, if the team prefers, to submit targeted credits for review entirely at the end of the project. Conversely, Green Globes is a matrix of categories, stages, and phases, fundamentally resulting in a separate checklist for each project phase, from project initiation through schematic design and on to commissioning—eight phases in all—resulting in a compilation of eight checklists.

As an example: LEED defines one end goal as using materials with recycled content for 10% of the building's material cost; however, LEED does not tell you what path to take to get there, although it does give suggestions. Similarly, NAHB outlines the end goal for incorporating recycled content and provides various strategies that may help the project's cause. Green Globes, on the other hand, begins asking the team questions during the project planning process to help ensure that the design team is addressing the appropriate issues as the project takes shape, without specifically outlining the end goal up front. While the various approaches employed by all three organizations provide valid means of guidance, they appear very different when one attempts (as we do in this book) to accurately compare specific elements of the systems, such as the treatment of materials. Nonetheless, understanding the structure and system context that underlie the various rating systems is an important foundation for moving forward with green material selection.

Common Material Credits

In addition to their structural differences, rating systems use different terminology to refer to various material standards. For example, Green Globes uses the phrase "Resources Systems Options & Building Material Selection." LEED, on the other hand, categorizes materials under "Materials and Resources." These sound—and are—remarkably similar, but behind the phrasing you will find that each rating system has a different method and theory to its approach.

By putting the term "Resources" first, Green Globes implies a broader view of the materials and their associations, such as life cycle assessment and embodied energy. While these issues are more difficult to quantify (although progress has been made on this front, which will be addressed later in this chapter), they are also an indication of where green building as a movement is going. Similarly, NAHB's Standards address "Resource Efficiency," suggesting a similar umbrella. The LEED rating system emphasizes "Materials" themselves, reflected in the emphasis on thresholds for credit achievement—thresholds based on the dollar amount of materials used on the project.

Because little variation exists as to *how* to include sustainable materials in your design and building processes, you'll find common material themes across the different rating systems. These recurring themes include large-scale issues such as the reuse of existing buildings or materials for your project, or more specific criteria such as locally available materials and products that make use of recycled content. While the various rating systems may word them differently, essentially they address the same concerns.

For example, regarding the use of locally available materials, the LEED rating system has a credit—Credit 5—clearly titled "Regional Materials" in their Materials and Resources section. *(Note that when we refer to the LEED rating system, we are referencing the most recent version, LEED Version 3.0. However, all rating systems, standards, and guidelines are changing rapidly, so please check the most updated version of each system for specifics.)* The LEED rating system specifically designates a 500-mile radius for a material to qualify as "regional." Green Globes, on the other hand, asks you to describe the local materials that are being used and to provide the specifications. NAHB's Standards address the possibility of local and regional material use in their Innovative Options section under "Resource Efficiency." Here, no credit is offered for the use of local materials, but doing so could effectively be included as a bonus.

As you can see from this example, while each of the rating systems addresses the use of local and regional materials within projects, they each approach it very differently. However, the intentions are the same: (a) to use local materials in order to minimize transportation costs and the energy consumed in getting the material from its source to the project site; and (b) to support the local economy.

Let's now take a look at how the different systems address recycled content. NAHB's *National Green Building Standard* (2008) reports that, "To obtain three base points, the project must have a minimum of two types of recycled-content material. Each additional type of recycled-content material used beyond this would give the project another point each, with a maximum of six points." This approach provides guidance on the number of recycled materials that need to be used, but the percentage of recycled content within the material is not addressed.

Green Globes, in its Construction Documents Questionnaire, asks, "Will building materials with recycled content be used in construction? Describe the types and quantities of recycled materials that will be integrated." The LEED system requires ". . . materials with recycled content such that the sum of post-consumer recycled content plus ½ of the pre-consumer recycled content constitutes at least 10% or 20%, based on cost, of the total value of the materials in the project." From this example, we can see that some rating systems take a quantitative approach to this material criterion, while others use a lighter touch. Some systems focus on the number of individual materials themselves; others focus on the content percentages within a given material.

Regarding the selection of wood in projects, a number of certifications exist, but they vary from one rating system to another. LEED, for example, has created a Certified Wood credit, seen in the Materials and Resources section as Credit 7. The credit reads that projects should "use a minimum of 50% (based on cost) of wood-based materials and products that are certified in accordance with the Forest Stewardship Council's principles and criteria, for wood building components. These components include, at a minimum, structural framing and general dimensional framing, flooring, sub-flooring, wood doors, and finishes." The LEED rating system currently sticks to one certification system as its standard, citing only the Forest Stewardship Council (FSC; www.fsc.org) as the organization to reference. Remember that this could change at any time, so be sure to check the most recent version of the rating system(s) you decide to use for any updates.

NAHB's Standards contain similar considerations for including wood from responsibly managed forests, but it has a longer list of acceptable certification bodies. The Standards state that projects should "use certified wood for wood and wood-based materials and products from all credible third-party–certified sources, including The Sustainable Forestry Initiative Program, The American Tree Farm System, The Canadian Standards Association's Sustainable Forest Management System Standards (CAN/SA Z809), the Forest Stewardship Council, the Program for the Endorsement of Forest Certification Systems (PEFC), and other such credible programs as they are developed and implemented."

Green Globes takes a similar tack in its Systems and Materials Selection in the Construction Documents Stage by asking "Do the construction documents specify that tropical hardwoods will not be used and that solid lumber and timber panel products will originate from certified and sustainable sources (i.e., Sustainable Forestry Initiative, CSA, Forestry Steward-ship Council, American Tree Farm System)?" As you can see, they also list a number of viable certification bodies and suggest that others not listed would also be acceptable. This topic is one example of how different systems may treat different material topics more or less stringently depending on the individual system's approach, underlying philosophies, and target audiences.

While we will address life cycle assessment (LCA) in more depth in Chapter 4, for now, let's simply define it as the total cost and impact of a given material with respect to the environment, cost, energy, waste, and so forth. LCA is a complex issue. It is difficult to define and quantify, and for that reason, the rating systems have found incorporating LCA to be challenging.

The NAHB Standard, for example, identifies LCA as one of the major steps in its development process. Within the Standard itself, however, LCA is mentioned in the Innovative Options category of the Resource Efficiency section.

Similarly, the newly established LEED credit weightings address LCA, but it is not called out specifically in a particular credit. Rather, life cycle issues have been incorporated into the structure of every LEED credit where LCA is applicable. This approach is reflected by the available points for each credit, although LCA is not specifically mentioned or assigned a quantifiable value in LEED's Resources—Systems and Materials Selection section.

For its part, Green Globes inquires in the Construction Documents Questionnaire, "Are materials from renewable sources and/or locally manufactured materials specified, and have these undergone a life cycle assessment?" While this does not set standards as to what life cycle tool to use, and combines LCA with the other tangential issues of renewable and local materials, Green Globes is signaling a shift in thinking from individual attributes to a more holistic evaluation found in life cycle assessment.

In addition to the issues already mentioned regarding where and how new materials are secured, reusing existing materials also offers significant benefits and is widely recognized in most building standards. Materials that have already been harvested and manufactured not only slow the depletion of resources, but also eliminate the pollution and energy associated with extraction. For example, recycling aluminum saves 95% of the energy needed to produce new aluminum from raw materials.[1] This energy expenditure during extraction, transportation, and manufacturing is commonly referred to as *embodied energy*.

Choosing to use an existing building for a new project is a great example of the integral role that material (re)use plays in the life cycle discussion. Think about the magnitude of the potential impact that can be reduced or eliminated when you take into consideration the scale of the building, all the materials that go into it, and all the resources and energy that go into them. Making use of an existing building not only eliminates the need for new material, it keeps a considerable amount of demolition debris from being routed to the landfill and prevents the resource expenditure required to modify them for reuse. If materials are providing a useful structure or space as they are—and can meet the project's demands in their current form as a building—why not leave them?

Green Globes does not address the idea of building reuse specifically, but does give a nod to it in the Resources, Building Material, and Solid Waste section of the Pre-Design: Site Analysis Questionnaire. Specifically, Green Globes asks "Where

> *Embodied energy* is the total energy needed for a product to live out its life cycle from beginning to end (i.e., cradle to grave) or beginning to a new beginning (cradle to cradle). This compilation includes the energy used in the raw material extraction; transportation from the extraction site to the manufacturing location; the manufacturing process itself; any associated assembly or installation; and, finally, energy expended in the product's deconstruction and/or decomposition. Embodied energy is, therefore, all the energy spent in the total life cycle of the product.

there are existing structures, have various options been assessed to retain or retrofit them?" This approach does not appear to emphasize an intentional, a priori choice to select a site where a reusable structure is present; rather, it simply asks that if buildings already exist on the chosen site, what, if any, consideration was given to their potential reuse. As a result, the Green Globes standard does not seem to take a proactive stance with respect to site selection; indeed it leaves the feeling that the site could have been selected despite the existence of buildings on it.

However, the Green Globes questionnaires do evolve throughout the process and, by the time you reach the Design Development Stage, the questions morph into a subcategory under "Strategies to reuse parts of the existing building." One question asks, "In the case of a fully renovated building, what percentage of the existing façades will be used?" and provides selections for less than 50%, at least 50%, at least 75%, 100%, or N/A. Green Globes also asks, "Are 50% of the existing major structures (other than the shell) being reused?"

In contrast, LEED specifically asks if an existing building has been selected to house the program, thus eliminating the need for new construction. Now located appropriately in the Materials & Resources section in LEED Version 3.0, the intent of the credit is "to extend the life cycle of existing building stock, conserve resources, retain cultural resources, reduce waste, and reduce environmental impacts of new buildings as they relate to materials manufacturing and transport." Percentage thresholds (55%, 75%, and 95%) indicate the extent to which this credit is achieved, rewarding the project for reducing its need for new construction. LEED also offers an additional credit for reuse of not just the exterior shell, but the interior non-structural elements as well.

NAHB's Standards are geared toward the home building industry, so they address only site selection in terms of environmental criteria (brownfield development, flood plains, etc.) rather than retrofitting existing structures. Since NAHB's members are primarily involved in new home construction, reusing existing buildings is not at the forefront of their interests.

The same underlying themes we have just reviewed regarding LCA, building reuse, and demolition waste can also be seen at a different scale in the issue of *material* reuse. While the underlying premise is the same, material reuse—as opposed to building reuse—looks at the materials as individual parts.

LEED has a specific credit attributed to this issue and will grant one or two points to the project depending on how much salvaged, refurbished, or reused material is used in the project: 5% or 10% based on the total value of materials within the project. Similarly, NAHB's Standards dedicate Section 2.3 in their Resource Efficiency section to Reuse Materials. However, while LEED's credits speak directly to the amount of material being used in the new project, NAHB's Section 2.3.2 only speaks to the general use of salvaged material, complementing two other line items under this heading that deal with deconstruction and sorting construction waste. In LEED, the credits associated with construction waste and sorting of debris are housed under a the Construction Waste Management section is distinctly separate from materials that are being installed in the project as structural elements or final finishes that will remain in the completed product. Green Globes takes a similar approach to that of LEED, asking "Will used building materials and components be integrated in the construction?" They also ask about materials that will be kept on site, and not how those materials that are removed from the site will be treated.

As you can see from this comparison, Green Globes and LEED primarily emphasize the materials that will be used in the project, while considering the issue of waste management separately. Although the NAHB Standards also address reclaimed and salvaged material, they puts more emphasis on the material leaving the site and how that material may be reused on another project.

Another item worth noting is that all green building guidelines encourage the use of renewable materials. In our discussions above on life cycle assessment, we noted that Green Globes incorporates the issue of renewable materials by partnering it with life cycle considerations and the use of local resources in both the Design Development Questionnaire and in the Construction Documents Stage. In the Green Globes' Design Development Questionnaire, the issue of renewable materials is treated rather substantially in a section entitled "Strategies to minimize the use of non-renewable resources." The five separate line items within that section address many of the specific topics covered thus far, including certified wood, recycled content, and local materials; also included is a question about durability, which is not found in any other green building guidelines. In the Construction Documents Stage, Green Globes asks, "Are materials from renewable sources and/or locally manufactured materials specified, and have these undergone a life cycle assessment?" The phrasing of this question could be interpreted as diluting the emphasis on renewable materials because it incorporates the issue of locally manufactured materials as well, but we do not believe that is what Green Globes intended in coupling the two together this way in the credits.

NAHB also has a separate section for renewable materials. It consists of two line items: one is about certified wood (covered earlier); the other requests the use of "materials manufactured from renewable resources or agricultural byproducts such as soy-based insulation, bamboo, or wood-based products." LEED also gives renewable materials their own credit, but with the further qualification of "Rapidly Renewable Materials." The thought behind this is that many materials are renewable—old growth trees are actually renewable, they just take a lot longer to replenish than we might like; hence the qualifier "rapidly" by which LEED means materials that will grow to maturity within ten years. Here again, LEED is looking for a threshold of material use based on total material cost of the project; in this case, that threshold is 2.5% (of the materials used should be rapidly renewable, replacing non-renewable materials or those with a long growth cycle).

Chemical Considerations

Other considerations pertaining to materials are typically found in the section of the guidelines covering the quality of the interior environment. In particular, they address what you might recognize as the "new car smell." That "wonderful" smell now sold as an air freshener scent is actually due to chemicals being released from all of the processed materials within the car—the upholstery, adhesives, carpeting, leather, and plastics—which were covered with plastic or trapped within the sealed car cab until it reached the lot. It is unlikely that much fresh air reached the interior of the car until it was purchased, allowing the chemicals to saturate the air within.

This smell occurs in buildings, too. Materials that are installed during construction have the ability to emit a whole host of chemical odors and contaminants that can be trapped within the building once completed. As our buildings have become tighter over the years due to improvements in energy efficiency and better techniques for sealing the building envelope, we've eliminated leaks and gaps in thresholds, ensuring a mechanically-induced comfortable environment. At the same time, we have also succeeded in sealing other unfavorable chemicals within our structures. Many of them are not necessarily strong, or really even noticeable, but in high concentrations they can cause sickness and headaches—and ultimately absentee days that result in unhappy employees and lower productivity for organizations.

Criteria for limiting or eliminating these noxious chemical effects are typically found in a category alluding to air testing. For Green Globes, that criteria is found in the Construction Documents Questionnaire under the Indoor Environment heading in the question, "Do the construction documents specify interior materials that are low-VOC emitting, non-toxic, and chemically inert?" VOCs (volatile organic compounds) are chemicals that become fumes as the material cures and can cause major health problems. Green Globes also addresses other indoor air criteria including the elimination of issues such as mold, sick building syndrome, and Legionella, but the Construction Documents Questionnaire is the only place in Green Globes that addresses the contribution of material selection to indoor air quality.

NAHB addresses the topic of indoor health thoroughly, since unhealthy homes can be a real problem in the marketplace. NAHB's Section 5: Indoor Environmental Quality contains a subsection dedicated to "Minimiz(ing) the potential source of pollutants." Here there are a number of line items that address materials such as low-VOC–emitting wallpaper, low formaldehyde emission standards for wood substrates, and "Green Label" qualifications for carpet, carpet pads, adhesives, and the like. Similarly, LEED addresses the issue in its section on Indoor Environmental Quality and has a series of credits on low-emitting materials. As subcategories, LEED includes adhesives and sealants, paints and coatings, flooring systems, and composite wood and agrifiber products. For each subcategory in LEED points can be achieved; thresholds are established for each subcategory in their specific application.

Summary

This overview clearly illustrates that there are strong and consistent material themes running throughout the world of green building guidelines. Issues such as local materials, renewable materials, recycled content, and material reuse are seen consistently across the guidelines, regardless of which specific guideline is being used. Other material considerations such as building reuse and life cycle assessment are not as prevalent, but are still present. Material considerations are emphasized, quantified, and valued to different degrees in different guidelines.

Throughout the rest of this book, we discuss the considerations for each of the primary materials categories, delineated earlier—structural, wall systems, floor systems, countertops, millwork, furniture, finishes—enabling individuals and teams to understand what they should be looking for when selecting materials for projects. There is room for a lot of give and take, and many shades of "green" exist. Our goal is to provide you with a framework that can both inform and help you simplify the sustainable material selection process.

Chapter 2: Overarching Considerations

Selecting materials, whether for commercial, institutional, or residential application, has always entailed balancing these considerations:

- **Performance:** A material must meet the performance requirements for the specific installation according to applicable building code, germ resistance, fire rating, etc.
- **Durability:** A material must last for a substantial amount of time without needing to be replaced, thereby reducing waste sent to the landfill.
- **Price:** A material must meet the project's budget constraints, understanding that each building material has industry standards that can be achieved at different price points.
- **Aesthetics:** A material must provide the "look" and the appearance characteristics important to the project's overall design.

To these considerations, "go green" and the goal of sustainability can now be added to the equation. As the industry introduces more and more green building products, we have learned that to be successful, a green product must meet the foundational requirements *and* offer the sustainable features that are becoming increasingly important. No matter how "green" a product might be, if it does not perform, if it is not affordable, or if it is just plain ugly, it will not sell. It takes a balance of these attributes to create a successful green product.

The most frequent objection to introducing sustainability to a common product is the assumption that this "greening" feature will add significantly to the product's cost. In fact, in many cases it does not. If a premium does exist for green products, it is often a matter of supply and demand economics. Consider this: The early innovators of green products tended to be small manufacturers who had a novel idea they wanted to bring to market. Their size created an inherent limitation in terms of scale. A small manufacturer has a significant amount of overhead in introducing a single product to an emerging market, whereas a more established incumbent can spread those same costs over more products, or use existing marketing efforts and channels to introduce new product lines. As more sustainable products are introduced and more commonly used, the costs associated with purchase, fabrication, and installation decrease. We have already seen a leveling of the playing field with the cheaper, non-green predecessors. For example, ten years ago when bamboo flooring was introduced as an alternative to wood floors, limited manufacturing capacity made the cost very high. Now that bamboo flooring production is commercial, the cost is equal to or less than traditional wood floors.

The increased demand for green products has created confusion about what is really green. With the industry still evolving, little consensus has yet to emerge on what, exactly, constitutes green, sustainable, or eco-friendly. Definitions of green and sustainability vary drastically, and, currently, a lack of reliable sources to evaluate manufacturers' claims for their products make consensus even more difficult. No single tool or resource exists for evaluating products—indeed such a tool would be difficult to develop due to the range of products, environmental issues, and chemical concerns for various categories of products. You might be left feeling that selecting green materials has become more of an art than a science.

The tremendous motivation for companies to market their products as "green" has led to unverifiable claims, a proliferation of unreliable labels, and just basic bad information, further complicating the situation. The term "greenwashing"—reflecting consumers' sentiments and lack of trust—has surfaced in the industry to refer to this type of misleading situation.

Several industry groups and nonprofit organizations are working diligently to standardize definitions of green, certify various aspects of products, develop rating systems, and inject more transparency into the raw materials and manufacturing processes involved in the production of building materials. Despite these efforts, confusion reigns, with various labels making vastly different claims.

Until a single industry standard emerges (if one ever does), confusion about what the "right" choices are will likely continue. As noted earlier, certain guidelines and standards may be more suitable for a particular project than others. Architects, designers, and specifiers can select the building standard or rating system that most closely aligns with their objectives and those of their project partners.

With that as prologue, we will turn our attention now to outlining criteria designed to assist you in selecting materials. Specifically, we will define the attributes that should be considered when evaluating green materials and relate these attributes to the rating systems we outlined in the previous chapter. We will also begin to define steps that move toward the wider thought process of life cycle assessment.

What Is "Green"?

While the terms "green," "sustainable," and "eco-friendly" have been used interchangeably in the past, they are becoming more refined as the industry evolves.

- *Green* has come to encompass issues of health and the impact on the environment in general.
- *Sustainable* builds on the health and environmental concerns of "green" by adding concerns related to social impacts, such as labor practices and fair trade.
- *Eco-friendly*, the broadest of these terms, generally refers to attributes that do not hurt the environment. Terms like "high recycled content," "recyclable," or even "natural/organic" (such as to describe stone) have been associated with this term.

For purposes of this book, we will focus on the health and environmental impacts and also explore some of the emerging issues and efforts related to social impacts.

Health Impacts

Unhealthy buildings have a significant impact on the productivity and satisfaction of tenants, and can present real risks for their owners. The Environmental Protection Agency (EPA) estimates that Americans spend up to 90% of their time indoors and that the indoor levels of pollutants can be two to five times—and sometimes as much as 100 times—higher than outside air.[2] Excessive levels of a single pollutant, or elevated levels of two or more such substances in combination, can lead to sick building syndrome. In a separate study, the EPA estimates that significant complaints of health problems caused by sick buildings are lodged against up to 30% of new and remodeled buildings.[3]

The costs associated with sick buildings were quantified in a study by the Harvard School of Public Health. That study indicated building-related illnesses account for $60 billion in lost productivity annually in the United States.[4] Working in collaboration, owners, architects, engineers, builders, and facilities managers can eliminate negative health effects, liability, bad publicity, and costly renovations associated with sick buildings.

So we ask: *How do buildings become "sick" in the first place?* Some common causes of sick buildings are lack of adequate ventilation, poor temperature control, and the presence of volatile organic compounds (VOCs) from material off-gassing.

Fresh, clean air is essential for efficient body and brain functioning. Ironically, as building structures have become more energy-efficient, less fresh air enters their interior environments. Walls, windows, and doors are very tightly sealed due to innovative construction techniques and materials that limit air flow, primarily to provide better temperature control and to minimize heating and cooling costs. Buildings are essentially "sealed shut" for energy efficiency; this, unfortunately, can lead to the circulation of dirty and polluted air within the building.

To address this problem—and to create a balance between energy efficiency and healthy indoor air quality—new air handling systems have been developed to bring in fresh air, condition that air, and then circulate it throughout the building. In fact, the American Society of Heating, Refrigerating, and Air-Conditioning Engineers (ASHRAE) recently increased requirements for the amount of outdoor air that must be supplied to a building according to the number of occupants in the building.

Most indoor air pollution comes from sources inside the building. Adhesives, carpeting, upholstery, manufactured wood products, and cleaning agents may all emit VOCs. VOCs can cause chronic and acute health problems. Some are known carcinogens. The existence of indoor contaminants has resulted in many complaints related to building environments and employee health. These concerns, in combination with other factors such as inadequate temperature, humidity, or lighting, all affect overall employee health and, ultimately, workplace productivity.

Healthy interiors have become a major focus of green building rating systems, legislation for schools and government buildings, and a primary concern for employees and employers alike. Consider these two recent studies that verify the benefits of healthy indoor air quality, the first study by William Fisk, the second by the University of San Diego:

- In 2000, William Fisk, senior staff scientist and department head of the Indoor Environment Department at the Lawrence Berkeley National Laboratory, wrote a comprehensive study examining the literature on green building and the health and productivity of occupants. The major finding of the study was that "for the United States, the estimated potential annual savings and productivity gains are:
  - $6 to $14 billion from reduced allergies and asthma,
  - $10 to $30 billion from reduced sick building syndrome symptoms, and
  - $20 to $160 billion from direct improvements in worker performance due to green building that are unrelated to health."[5]

The study emphasized that these savings, though often overlooked, are very important because the potential savings from productivity gains are a much larger portion of an employer's budget than other costs, and are larger, for example, than the total estimated cost of energy used in buildings. Even at the lower ranges, these savings represent a tangible impact on an organization's bottom line.

- A 2009 study from the University of San Diego demonstrated that LEED-certified buildings provide more productive environments for workers than non-green buildings. The study shows gains of over $6,000 per employee per year—that is, productivity gains (including fewer sick days) of more than 6% per employee.[6]

These studies verify theories on the correlation between healthy indoor air quality and productivity. That's good news all around, not only for tenants, but also for owners and developers looking for data that support the idea that going green can contribute significantly to a building's ROI (return on investment).

Indoor Air Quality: Eliminating Common Pollutants

Indoor Air Quality (IAQ) is a concern for new and old buildings alike. New buildings may have the latest ventilation systems yet still suffer from off gassing of new materials such as carpet, paint, adhesives, and other common interior finishes. Many older buildings and retrofits seek Energy Star certification. While these buildings likely have upgraded to more energy-efficient HVAC systems, they should go beyond Energy Star requirements and consider improvements in indoor air quality via new ventilation and air exchange systems as well as careful materials selection and finishes to minimize the introduction of toxic compounds and VOCs.

All materials can be placed on an environmental impact continuum, affecting human health and the environment to varying degrees. A wide range of environmental health policies promulgated by local and national governments, as well as those created by international treaties, have identified a set of chemicals that, due to their high toxicity and global impact, warrant priority efforts to eliminate their use.

The Healthy Building Network (HBN; www.healthybuilding.net) was founded in 2000. This organization works in the building sector to move the industry away from materials that incorporate what are known as "worst in class" chemicals toward alternatives that are currently understood to be safer. HBN has identified the following high priority, worst in class chemicals.

Persistent Bioaccumulative Toxics

Persistent Bioaccumulative Toxics (PBTs) are at the top of the worst in class chemicals list. PBTs do not break down readily from natural processes. They accumulate in fatty tissues, becoming more concentrated as they move up the food chain (and thus, bioaccumulative). Furthermore, they are generally highly toxic in small quantities, creating a toxic legacy that will haunt us potentially for decades to come. Hence, environmental health advocates emphasize the importance of substituting green products for materials whose manufacture, use, and disposal result in the release of PBTs into the environment. Building materials that release PBTs include polyvinyl chloride (PVC)–based products, mercury thermometers, lead solders, roofing materials, and certain paints and finishes, to name the most common.

Phasing Toxics Out of Building Materials

As the green building movement moves forward and awareness heightens, a number of harmful substances are being phased out of materials and manufacturing. While all materials may be on their way to becoming more environmentally friendly, below you'll find a brief discussion of the specific substances (along with key issues attendant to them and suggested alternatives) that we encourage you to pay particular attention to as you consider material possibilities for your project:

- Phthalates
- Heavy Metals
- Halogenated Flame Retardants (HFRs)
- Perfluorocarbons (PFCs)
- Polyvinyl Chloride (PVC)
- Formaldehyde and Urea Formaldehyde
- Volatile Organic Compounds (VOCs)

Phthalates

Phthalates are used as plasticizers to soften polyvinyl chloride plastic, also known as PVC or vinyl, including a wide range of building products such as vinyl flooring, wall covering, and upholstery.

Phthalate plasticizers are not chemically bound to PVC. They have been found to leach, migrate or evaporate into indoor air and atmosphere, food, and other materials. Human exposure occurs through direct contact and use, indirectly through leaching into other products, or general environmental contamination.

In October 2007, California joined the European Union in restricting the use of phthalates in the use of children's products. In August 2008, the U.S. Congress passed the Consumer Product Safety Improvement Act (CPSIA) that restricts the manufacture, sale, or import of children's products that contain certain phthalates. However, because phthalates are not a volatile organic compound (VOC), they are usually not accounted for by indoor air quality standards, such as those used to certify green building materials.

Phthalates, along with two other known human carcinogens—vinyl chloride and dioxin— are associated with PVC. These three chemicals present a triple threat, making PVC perhaps the worst possible plastic for use in buildings from an environmental health and green building perspective. Regrettably, there are still few restrictions on the use of vinyl in green buildings. (More about PVC later in this chapter.)

You'll rarely find the word "phthalates" on a label (except for the occasional "phthalate-free," which is helpful). However, thedailygreen.com lists three tips for identifying products that have, or are likely to have phthalates:

(1) Read the ingredients. You can identify phthalates in some products by their chemical names, or abbreviations:

- DBP (di-n-butyl phthalate) and DEP (diethyl phthalate) are often found in personal care products, including nail polishes, deodorants, perfumes and cologne, aftershave lotions, shampoos, hair gels, and hand lotions. (BzBP, see below, is also in some personal care products.)
- DEHP (di-2-ethylhexyl) phthalate or Bis (2-ethylhexyl phthalate) is used in PVC plastics, including some medical devices. BzBP (benzylbutyl phthalate) is used in some flooring, car products, and personal care products. DMP (dimethyl phthalate) is used in insect repellent and some plastics (as well as rocket propellant).

(2) Be wary of the term "fragrance." It is often used to denote a combination of compounds, possibly including phthalates, which are a subject of recent concern because of studies showing they can mimic certain hormones.

(3) Choose plastics with the recycling code 1, 2 or 5. Recycling codes 3 and 7 are more likely to contain phthalates.[7]

Heavy Metals

The use of heavy metals such as lead, mercury, and chromium in building products lead to the release of toxics into the environment during extraction, production, use, and disposal.

Lead and mercury are potent neurotoxicants, particularly damaging to the brains of fetuses and growing children. The reliance on lead and mercury in the building industry has reduced significantly over the past twenty years, but lead continues to be used in some building materials. For example:

- Lead is used in flashing, copper and other roof products, solder, batteries, and in some PVC products such as wire insulation jacketing and exterior siding.
- Mercury can be found in thermostats, thermometers, switches, and fluorescent lamps.
- Chromium can be found in chrome or stainless steel components of furniture.
- Cadmium, cobalt, antimony trioxide, and other metals may be incorporated into paint, dyes and pigments, fabric, and some PVC products such as resilient flooring.

Product redesign is the most effective way to eliminate heavy metals from building products. *Look for products with no heavy metals.*

Halogenated Flame Retardants (HFRs)

Flame-retardants, used in fabrics, foams, and various other plastics have certainly saved many lives. However, those that are halogenated, including polybrominated diphenyl ethers (PBDE) and other brominated flame retardants (BFRs), have been used in a wide array of products, including building materials, electronics, furnishings, motor vehicles, airplanes, plastics, polyurethane foams, and textiles. The health hazards of these chemicals have attracted increasing scrutiny as they have been shown to disrupt thyroid and estrogen hormones, causing permanent changes to the brain and reproductive systems as well as reduced fertility. Being both persistent and bioaccumulative, HFRs are rapidly accumulating to dangerous levels in humans and are the subject of an increasing number of bans and phase-outs.

There are chemical alternatives available for HFRs and many alternatives exist for HFR applications in furniture, mattresses, draperies, foam, and other textiles applications. To accomplish this, companies have employed a range of green design strategies that include product redesign for better fire resistance, the use of inherently fire-resistant fibers and lightweight metals, and the substitution of brominated and chlorinated chemicals with safer alternatives. This has led to the development of new materials and chemicals that have a lower impact on human health and the environment.

Avoid products using any halogenated flame retardants.

Perfluorocarbons (PFCs)

This class of chemicals is widely used in air conditioning and the manufacturing of electronics, appliances, and carpets. In addition to their effects on human health, PFCs are also ozone depleting in certain forms. Scotchgard, Teflon, and Goretex—treatments for textiles (including carpet, apparel, and upholstery)—are all made with perfluorocarbons. When applied to fabrics, they provide stain resistance and water resistance.

Like HFRs, PFCs are highly persistent and bioaccumulative and can concentrate at alarming levels in humans and animals. Government scientists are especially concerned because unlike any other toxic chemicals, the most pervasive and toxic members of the PFC family never degrade in the environment and have been linked to a range of developmental and other adverse effects.

In January 2006, the EPA approached the eight largest fluorocarbon producers, requesting their participation in the 2010/15 PFOA Stewardship Program. The EPA also asked these producers to commit to reducing PFOA and related chemicals globally in both facility emissions and product content by 95% by 2010 and 100% by 2015.

Some changes that have occurred include the reformulation of Scotchgard based on perfluorobutane sulfonate, or PFBS. The company worked closely with the EPA and has performed more than forty studies, the results of which led to the conclusion that PFBS does not accumulate the way PFCs do. GreenShield finishes represent another step forward in PFC alternatives. GreenShield is a nanoparticle made of amorphous silica, an inert material that has well-established applications involving direct human consumption and is generally recognized as safe and approved by the Food and Drug Administration (FDA) and EPA for such applications. The use of silica enables GreenShield to reduce the amount of flurocarbons by a factor of 8.

The drastic reduction of PFC use in the textile industry is well underway and alternatives are being explored. However, additional research is still necessary to determine if the alternatives are safe for the environment and human health.

Avoid any product treated with a PFC-based material.

Polyvinyl Chloride (PVC)

According to Healthy Building Network, PVC is one of the most common synthetic materials used in construction.[8] PVC is a versatile resin and appears in thousands of different formulations and configurations. Over 14 billion pounds of PVC are currently produced per year in North America and over 30 million tons are produced globally each year.

The introduction of PVC as a wood replacement drove its rapid adoption as a building material, where it provides a relatively low cost, durable option that is weather-, mold-, moisture-, and pest-resistant. Approximately 75% of all PVC manufactured is used in construction materials, the most common of which are siding, pipe for drains, waste, and vent, resilient flooring, and window frames.

PVC has contributed a significant portion of the world's burden of persistent toxic pollutants and endocrine-disrupting chemicals—including dioxin and phthalates—that are now universally present in the environment and the human population. Posing hazards at each stage of its life cycle, PVC is dangerous from its manufacture through the end of its life, particularly at disposal. Due to the chemicals and additives in PVC, it cannot be recycled. Of an estimated 7 billion pounds of PVC thrown away in the U.S., only 14 million pounds—less than ½ of 1%—is recycled. The Association of Post-consumer Plastics Recyclers declared efforts to recycle PVC a failure and labeled it a contaminant in 1998.[9]

PVC has been singled out for elimination in many products because of the uniquely wide and potent range of chemicals it emits throughout its life cycle. PVC is virtually the only material that requires phthalate plasticizers, frequently includes heavy metals, and emits high levels of VOCs. In addition, during its manufacture PVC is responsible for the production of a large number of highly toxic chemicals including dioxins (the most potent carcinogens measured), vinyl chloride, ethylene dichloride, PCBs, and more. When burned at the end of its life, whether in an incinerator, structural fire, or landfill fire, vinyl releases hydrochloric acid and more dioxins.

While common rating systems such as LEED provide incentives for eliminating and reducing VOCs (discussed later) in several forms, PVC is also of great concern to environmentalists; yet, perhaps somewhat surprisingly, discussion of PVC is not widely incorporated into major rating systems.

That's not to say that the issue is not being looked at closely and seriously. After years of research, the U.S. Green Building Council (USGBC) issued a report in 2007 that verified the harmful effects of PVC, but ultimately concluded that to include a credit in the rating system that discouraged its use might encourage the use of even more harmful substitutes.[10] Instead, the report called for the use of Innovation & Design credits to encourage the industry to move forward by engaging the capabilities and motivation of the marketplace to find healthy alternatives to PVC. In late 2009, USGBC took further steps to encourage PVC alternatives by launching a new pilot credit for the elimination of persistent bioaccumulative toxic chemicals (PBTs), including PVC in building materials.

For reasons that should be obvious from the discussion of PVC, clearly the best choice is to avoid products made with PVC. For more info on PVC, see www.healthybuilding.net/pvc.

Avoid products made with PVC.

Formaldehyde and Urea Formaldehyde (UF)

Formaldehyde is found in the manufacture of many building materials and in a number of product finishes, such as sealants and coatings—all widely used in the construction industry. It is also used to add permanent-press qualities to fabrics and draperies, as a component of glues and adhesives, and as a preservative in some paints and coating products.

According to the EPA, the most significant sources of formaldehyde are pressed wood products made using adhesives that contain urea formaldehyde (UF) resins.[11] Pressed wood products made for indoor use include particleboard (used as sub-flooring, shelving, and in cabinetry and furniture); hardwood plywood paneling (used for decorative wall covering and in cabinets and furniture); and medium-density fiberboard (used for drawer fronts, cabinets, and furniture tops). Medium-density fiberboard contains a higher resin-to-wood ratio than any other pressed wood product and is generally recognized as being the highest formaldehyde-emitting pressed wood product. Other potential sources of formaldehyde in the home include cigarette smoke, clothes, upholstery and draperies, glues, paints and other coatings, and fiberglass insulation.

Formaldehyde is a colorless, pungent-smelling gas that can cause watery eyes, burning sensations in the eyes and throat, nausea, bronchial irritation, and is often associated with symptoms related to multiple chemical sensitivity syndromes. High concentrations may trigger attacks in people with asthma. Formaldehyde has been shown to cause cancer in animals and is suspected of causing cancer in humans. In fact, formaldehyde is so prevalent—and of such concern—that many governments and oversight organizations are classifying the chemical as a carcinogen and banning or significantly curbing its use, especially in the built environment.

Formaldehyde and urea formaldehyde both contribute to poor indoor air quality. Formaldehyde levels in the air increase noticeably when, for example, pressed wood products are used indoors. Urea formaldehyde has been particularly present in building materials because it can be manufactured at very low cost from easily available raw materials. Its use in outdoor construction materials is more limited as urea formaldehyde resin hydrolyzes (decomposes) in extremely humid conditions and at high temperatures.

Most rating systems seek to eliminate the use of urea formaldehyde in building products because it is the most harmful. These rating systems will refer to products that have "no-added urea formaldehyde" (NAUF). Alternatives to UF still contain other forms of formaldehyde. We can expect increased pressure to eliminate these other forms of formaldehyde and to move toward standard "no-added formaldehyde" (NAF). More research and development is needed to find comparable performance in a cost-effective alternative to formaldehyde-based products.

Urea formaldehyde is cheap and effective, which is why it is so commonly used in a number of materials. Mainstream product manufacturers have only recently been successful in developing materials with the same performance qualities as those using urea formaldehyde, without adding exorbitant manufacturing costs.

PSI Green Expectations, a monthly publication from Panel Source Inc. (now McKillican) published a brief article in December 2008 entitled, *Beyond Formaldehyde*. The article declared, "UF (urea formaldehyde) received its 'death sentence' in the mid-2000s as a result of two separate actions: the USGBC LEED program awarded a point to projects using panels made without UF Resins (EQ 4.4), and the California Air Resources Board (CARB) legislated a program to reduce formaldehyde emissions to extremely low levels—levels that UF resins are unlikely to achieve."[13] The article goes on to outline the following potential alternatives to UF resins:

- **Melamine Urea Formaldehyde:** The addition of melamine to UF resin results in improved moisture resistance and reduced emissions. However, it still contains UF as a component. Given that the industry is moving toward no-UF products, this is not a long-term alternative.

- **Phenol Formaldehyde (PF):** UF's distant cousin, this resin is the current go-to alternative for producers dropping UF from their toolboxes. However, PF isn't always popular because the resin is expensive, takes a long time to cure, and often darkens the material in which it is used (due to longer curing times). PF can also result in "resin" spots appearing on the surface. PF's other handicap is the fact that the resin contains and emits formaldehyde. While the emissions are at very low concentrations, they are emissions nonetheless. The market senses that PF is being accepted by activists only because it is better than UF, but once UF is no longer used, PF will likely be the next target for elimination.

- **Polymeric Methylene Diphenyl Diisocyanate (pMDI):** The other commercially acceptable resin at this point, pMDI has some positive attributes. For example, the resin forms both a chemical and a physical bond, making the bonds far stronger than either UF or PF bonds. In addition, the resin is completely inert when cured, has a high degree of moisture resistance, cures quickly in a press, and is applied at very small addition levels. Of course, some drawbacks also exist. Compared to either UF or PF, pMDI is very expensive and its high cost negates the advantage of smaller addition rates that the resin offers. In addition, a release agent must be used in the press; otherwise, the resin does a good job of gluing the press and the board together, permanently! Finally, while the resin is inert when cured, the process of manufacturing the resin is anything but environmentally friendly, with a litany of carcinogenic compounds being used and created in the production of the resin itself.

Formaldehyde-Free Alternatives to Formaldehyde-based Resins

The most widely used completely formaldehyde-free alternative resins are MDI (methylene diphenyl isocyanate) and PVA (polyvinyl acetate). These resins have lower emissions but are derived from fossil fuels and can therefore still have toxic chemicals associated with their manufacture.

Soy-based resin technology has emerged in the last few years. It is being utilized as a binder in hardwood plywood panels. Currently the viscosity of the binder is too thick to be used in medium-density fiberboard and particle board manufacturing, where MDI is the best alternative. Soy-based adhesives have several benefits:

- Soy is a rapidly renewable resource.
- Soy has excellent mechanical properties that compete well with chemical-based alternatives.
- Soy as an alternative to formaldehyde has advantages in indoor air quality, workplace environmental safety, and ease of disposal.

- Soy-hyrolyzate and soy-flour adhesives do not require hazardous waste disposal.

Some companies leading the way in formaldehyde alternatives include:

- Sierra Pine Composite Solutions, which has a full line of NAUF particle board and a full line of NAF MDF (medium-density fiberboard; www.sierrapine.com).
- Columbia Forest Products, which first announced soy-based resins in 2006 when it launched PureBond, a cost-effective decorative plywood line (www.columbiaforestproducts.com).
- Smith & Fong, manufacturers of Plyboo bamboo products, which has used NAUF binders in their bamboo panels and flooring for years. In 2009, they announced the development of Soybond adhesive system to be phased into all of their products by 2010 (www.plyboo.com).

Volatile Organic Compounds (VOCs)

VOCs are an umbrella category of thousands of different chemicals, including familiar names such as formaldehyde and benzene, which evaporate readily into the air. VOCs are very common in traditional building materials. They are emitted as gases from certain solids and liquids and contribute to unhealthy interior air quality. VOCs are often found in paints and lacquers, glues and adhesives, particleboard, resilient flooring, carpeting, furnishings, and cleaning supplies, among others. These products can release organic compounds when installed, during use, and when they are stored. Off-gassing can occur for the lifetime of a product.

According to the EPA, VOCs can cause eye, nose, and throat irritation; headaches; loss of coordination; nausea; and damage to the liver, kidney, and central nervous system.[14] Some VOCs can cause cancer in animals; some are suspected or known to cause cancer in humans. Key signs or symptoms associated with exposure to VOCs include irritation, nose and throat discomfort, headache, allergic skin reaction, nausea, fatigue, and dizziness.

The building material categories most often associated with VOCs are products that contain formaldehyde, a common chemical in glues, resins, and solvents found in paints, adhesives, and other finishes, as discussed earlier. The following list and guidelines provide some of the common materials in which VOCs are found, and the certification bodies that test for low- or no-VOC-compliant products.

- *Wet Products (adhesives, paints, and other coatings):* Paints and finishes release low-level toxic emissions in the form of VOCs into the air for years after application. Until recently, the VOC-containing ingredients within the wet products were necessary to meet the performance requirements of the paint and the expectations of the customer.

New environmental regulations and consumer demand have led to the development of low-VOC and zero-VOC paints and finishes. Most paint manufacturers now produce one or more zero-VOC varieties of paint. These new paints are durable, cost-effective, and less harmful to human and environmental health. There are three general categories of paints that contain smaller amounts of VOCs; these will be discussed more fully in Chapter 11.

Seek no- or low-VOC products. Look for Green Seal certified paints or paints with less than 20 g/l VOCs and SCAQMD (South Coast Air Quality Management District) compliant adhesives and coatings.

• *Flooring, Carpeting, Wall Covering, Ceiling Tiles, and Furniture:* A variety of programs utilize the CA 01350 testing protocol to measure the actual levels of individual VOCs emitted from the material and compare them to allowable levels set by the state of California. These include CHPS, CRI's Green Label Plus, SCS's Indoor Advantage, RFCI's FloorScore, and GreenGuard's Schools & Children (see sidebar about CA 01350). It is best to avoid flooring that requires waxing and stripping as these processes will ultimately release more VOCs over the lifetime of the product than the original material.

Seek CA 01350 compliant products.

• *Composite Wood Products and Insulation:* The CA 01350 program sets limits on formaldehyde emissions, but for these products there are also options available with no formaldehyde added at all.

Look for products with no added formaldehyde.

Health Impact Conclusions

Poor indoor air quality is an area where architects, designers, and specifiers have great control, as they can choose materials that eliminate common pollutants that give off VOCs. Eliminating harmful compounds from a building interior should be a priority in a building project. Various studies have shown over and over how the elimination of such compounds can add dollars to the company bottom line by increasing productivity. The consideration of the healthy interior begins by looking at the overall air distribution system, then the air that is circulated, and, finally, what compounds exist within it. Eliminating VOCs is a critical first step in reducing the volume of compounds that are widely known to be unhealthy in an enclosed space. The following steps will guide you in addressing this issue in your projects:

- Use products with the lowest VOC content to minimize the overall health risk.
- Consider the amount of solids or pigments in paints, which can range in concentration from 25% to 45% by volume. The higher the percent solids, the fewer VOCs are in the paint.
- Avoid products that are registered with the EPA, OSHA, or DOT. Registration means that the product contains toxic ingredients that must be monitored due to potential harmful impacts on the environment and the applicator.
- Wherever possible, eliminate heavy metals, halogenated flame retardants, and perfluorocarbons, and inquire with product reps about their use in manufacturing.

To help galvanize the industry toward healthier alternatives, USGBC launched a pilot credit in late 2009 meant to "reduce the release of persistent bioaccumulative toxic chemicals (PBTs) associated with the life cycle of building materials." This pilot credit is attempting to address many of the health-related issues discussed in this chapter. To achieve this LEED credit, you must use materials manufactured without added halogenated organic compounds for at least 75% (by cost) of the material totals in a minimum of three of the following four groups:

- Exterior components (including, at a minimum, roof membranes, waterproofing membranes, window and door frames, and siding).
- Interior finishes (including, at a minimum, flooring, base, ceiling tiles, wall coverings, and window treatments).
- Piping, conduit, and electrical boxes.
- Building-installed electrical cable and wire jacketing.

This includes all plastics containing chlorine or fluorine, including PVC. It also includes all brominated and halogenated flame retardants (BFRs and HFRs). Alternative materials suggested include several forms of modified bitumen for roof membranes; natural linoleum, rubber, or alternate polymers for flooring and surfacing; natural fibers, polyethylene, polyester and paint for wall covering; polyethylene for wire and cable jacketing; wood, fiberglass, HDPE, and aluminum with thermal breaks for windows; steel, HDPE, and fiberglass for conduit; and copper, steel, concrete, clay, polypropylene, and HDPE for piping. Similarly, LEED also recommends that cast iron pipe should be avoided based on air quality concerns associated with manufacturing practices.

We don't dispute that some of the safety, fire resistance, and overall performance factors of some of the chemicals listed in this chapter have been improved. Other chemicals in this chapter (such as formaldehyde resins and PVC) fueled the

CA 01350 Is the Basis for Most VOC Standards and Certifications

California 01350 is a standard specification developed by the state of California to address key environmental performance issues related to the selection and handling of building materials. The standard represents a significant step forward in specifications designed to evaluate and reduce the impact of building materials on indoor air quality and health in buildings.

Initially developed in 2007 for a model office building project in Sacramento, the protocol and associated specification have subsequently gained popularity with green building advocates for their comprehensiveness and effectiveness in improving indoor air quality. As CA 01350's use has spread, it has become a major driving force for better products and healthier buildings. This is due, in part, to CA 01350's very clear and consistent protocol for manufacturers to test their products and reformulate accordingly to reduce emissions of troublesome chemicals below CA 01350's mandated levels.

Key elements that affect indoor air quality are identified in the specification for screening building materials (primarily major interior finishes) based on the following criteria:

- emissions testing protocol
- hazardous content screening and avoiding
- mold and mildew from construction practices

The specification language contained in CA 01350 has been integrated into other broader specification programs, including:

- Scientific Certification Systems (www.scscertified.com/iaq)
- Indoor Advantage Indoor Air Quality Performance Environmental Certification Program
- Environmentally Preferable Purchasing (EPP) carpet specification
- Resilient Floor Covering Institute's FloorScore
- Green Guide for Health Care (www.gghc.org)
- U.S. Green Building Council's LEED (www.usgbc.org)
- Collaborative for High Performance Schools Best Practices (www.CHPS.net)
- Institute for Market Transformation to Sustainability (MTS) SMART standards (http://MTS.sustainable-products.com)
- Carpet & Rug Institute's Green Label Plus Carpet Testing Program (www.carpet-rug.com)
- California's Reference Specifications for use in all major state construction (www.ciwmb.ca.gov/greenbuilding/Specs/Section01350)
- GreenGuard (www.greenguard.org)
- Green Label Plus (www.carpet-rug.org)

incredible growth in the building industry over the last several decades with low cost, durable products.

But—and this is a very big but—they are also known toxins with very real and very serious health effects. Now that we have a greater understanding of the impact of these chemicals on human health and the environment, we must seek alternatives, advocate for regulation of these chemicals, and push manufactures to develop new, innovative, and cost-effective solutions.

Environmental Concerns and Opportunities

The built environment has an enormous impact on the natural environment. Globally, buildings use 40% of raw materials (3 billion tons annually).[15] In the U.S. alone, consider that:

- Buildings are one of the heaviest consumers of natural resources and account for 38% of the greenhouse gas emissions (CO_2) that affect climate change.[16]
- Buildings represent almost 40% of energy use (includes fuel input for production).[17]
- Buildings represent 72% of U.S, consumption of electricity.[18]
- Buildings use almost 15% of all potable water (approximately 15 trillion gallons per year).[19]
- According to EPA estimates, 170 million tons of building-related construction and demolition debris were generated in 2003, with 61% coming from non-residential and 39% from residential sources.[20]
- The EPA further estimates that 209.7 million tons of municipal solid waste were generated in a single year.[21]

What does this mean for the building industry? Clearly, every decision we make influences these statistics. In this section, we will focus on selecting building materials that:

- Reduce waste (reclaimed or recycled);
- Conserve natural resources (rapidly renewable, sustainably harvested); and
- Reduce carbon output (local, life cycle of product).

Reducing Waste

Currently, the typical manufacturing system has open, linear material flows that take in materials and energy to create products and waste, then throw most of the waste away. Not much is recycled back into the manufacturing stream. Buildings make the single biggest impact on this cycle; this impact is the cumulative result of waste generated, the materials used to construct it, and the operation of the building, including electricity and water. The Zero Waste Alliance, a non-profit devoted to helping organizations implement sustainable solutions, demonstrates this cycle with a material

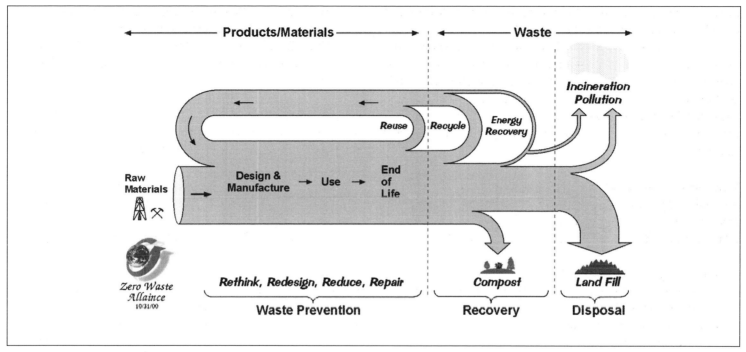

Figure 2.1. Material flows today. (Reproduced with permission of Zero Waste Alliance.)

flows diagram (Figure 2.1).[22] Notice the amount of raw materials and energy going into the system with very little being reused, recycled, or recovered. The vast majority of material ends up in the landfill.

Ideally, production systems would be cyclical and form a closed loop, as in nature, where there is no waste and materials remain completely contained in the production cycle, as illustrated in Figure 2.2.

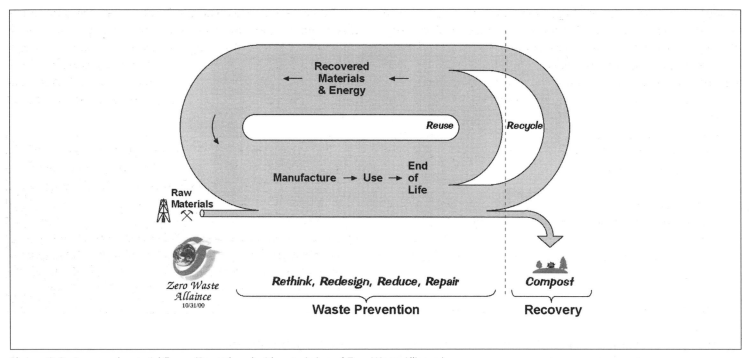

Figure 2.2. Improved material flows. (Reproduced with permission of Zero Waste Alliance.)

In addition to the environmental benefits, reduced waste leads to increased efficiency and lower costs. With these benefits in mind, several corporate alliances and initiatives have emerged to fundamentally redesign the manufacture of products and materials to eliminate harmful chemicals, optimize clean energy, reduce water consumption, and eliminate waste.

Architect William McDonough and his co-author, chemist Michael Braungart, make a powerful case for redesigning manufacturing to achieve those goals in their book, *Cradle to Cradle*.[23] The book calls for the transformation of industry through intelligent design—eliminating the current industrial system of "takes, makes, and wastes" to a manufacturing process that generates ecological, social, and economic value.

Taking the concept from theory to practice, the co-authors created a product certification program by the same name, Cradle to Cradle Certification[24] (see p. 71). The certification requires manufacturers to use environmentally safe and healthy materials, and to design for:

- material reutilization, such as recycling or composting;
- the use of renewable energy and energy efficiency; and
- the efficient use of water and maximum water quality associated with production.

Cradle to Cradle also calls for instituting strategies for social responsibility.

This type of thinking—that is, the application of intelligent design—moves the industry from thinking about building products that either pass or fail in terms of their environmental effects, to thinking that entails a broader understanding of all effects a product can have throughout its life cycle. Cradle to Cradle is discussed more fully in Chapter 3 and life cycle and life cycle thinking are covered more fully in Chapter 4.

Other ways in which you can identify materials that reduce waste are to look for companies and manufacturers with active commitments to energy management, water management, recycling, and the reuse of by-products, as well as those who purchase only what is needed for the project. Also consider companies that actively return, donate, or recycle unused materials.

Cradle-to-grave is a life cycle assessment of a product that considers its environmental impacts from the manufacturing phase (the "cradle") through its use and, ultimately, disposal phase (the "grave").

Cradle-to-cradle is also a full, life cycle assessment of a product, but goes one step further than the "cradle to grave" approach by examining the potential of a product to be reused or recycled—its rebirth, so to speak.

Conserving Natural Resources

When we discuss the life cycle of common building materials (in Chapter 5), you'll discover that the sourcing, extracting, and processing of raw materials has the greatest impact on the environment (compared to other life cycle stages such as transportation and product use). Some choices you can make to reduce these larger impacts include using materials that are:

- Recycled,
- Reclaimed,
- Rapidly renewable, or
- Certified as using sustainable or well-managed harvesting practices.

Using Recycled Materials

Recycling involves processing used materials into new products to prevent waste on a number of levels: (a) reducing the waste of potentially useful materials; (b) reducing the consumption of fresh raw materials; (c) reducing energy usage; (d) reducing air pollution (from incineration) and water pollution (from landfilling); and (e) lowering greenhouse gas emissions as compared to those emitted during virgin production.

Common recycled content used in building materials include plastic, glass, porcelain, paper, aluminum, steel, metal, and previously used stone and marble. Putting materials into the recycling bin is the easiest part of the process. From there, materials need to be collected, transported, sorted, cleaned, and reprocessed into a form that is suitable for manufacturing.

In an ideal system, materials would be recycled into a fresh supply of the same material. However, the infrastructure and technology needed to achieve this goal does not always exist,

is not 100% efficient, or is too expensive. Therefore, most recyclable materials are downcycled— that is, made into a product of lesser quality.

End-of-Life Possibilities for a Material

At the end of a product's useful life, it can be reused, upcycled, downcycled, recycled, or dumped in a landfill. Reusing and dumping are self-evident terms; here's what the others mean:

- ***Upcycling*** extracts components of the product and turns them back into virgin materials that can be used to make any other product.
- ***Downcycling*** is the recycling of a product into a product of lesser quality—for example, plastics being recycled into lower grade plastics.
- ***Recycling*** is reprocessing the product to produce the same end product.

Nevertheless, buying recycled products is an essential part of making recycling work (closing the loop). The residential building industry can play a major role in helping to reduce waste and promote recycling by specifying and asking for recycled products.

Some people are critical of the use of recycled materials. Their objections typically include the following:

- Some recycled materials, certain plastics in particular, use more resources and generate more pollution than do virgin materials. However, there are also many materials that, when recycled, offer clear benefits in terms of reducing the amount of energy and natural resources consumed, the pollutants released, and the landfill space used.
- Where is the "garbage crisis"? In the U.S. it is true that we still have space to throw our trash, but in Europe and other smaller, densely populated countries around the globe, room became scarce decades ago. The U.S. can learn a lesson here. In addition, this argument assumes that environmental impacts from storing garbage (contaminated soil, water, etc.) are minimal, and we already know that assumption is false.
- Jobs created by the recycling industry are a poor trade for the jobs lost in logging, mining, and other industries associated with virgin production. Although this position is purely subjective, an important point stands to be made: many problems still need to be solved in the recycling industry, and they point to opportunities for technology development, entrepreneurial endeavors, and new job creation.

However, when we examine some of the facts about recycling (see the sidebar), it's hard to ignore the significant, tangible benefits. You'll probably be surprised as you read them. See how many you already know!

Reclaiming Materials

Reusing building materials is one of the most sustainable activities that we, in the construction industry, can choose to do. We can deconstruct buildings in such a way that the materials (joists, flooring, siding, fixtures, and more) can be reused for new construction, thereby capitalizing on a cost-competitive alternative to conventional building demolition. By reusing building materials, we can achieve many environmental and social benefits, chief among them:

- Reducing the consumption of new resources;
- Minimizing landfill waste and pollution; and
- Creating value-added markets from waste materials.

Perhaps the most common example is reclaimed wood, which is a viable, cost-effective alternative to fresh-cut lumber. Most trees have a harvest age of at least twenty-five years and often over one hundred years. Deforestation is cited as one, if not the largest factor in increased CO_2 emissions, due to the ability of trees to absorb CO_2 from the environment. Two major efforts are underway to address this issue: one is to reduce the number and method of trees that are harvested (see the FSC discussion later); the other is to reduce the demand.

Facts About Recycled Materials

The Recycling Revolution (www.recycling-revolution.com) provides an extensive list of facts about recycling compiled from various sources, including the National Recycling Coalition, the Environmental Protection Agency, and Earth911.org. Here are some of the most significant:

Paper

- Recycling paper instead of making it from raw material generates 74% less air pollution, uses 50% less water, and requires 60% less energy.
- Approximately 1.5 million tons of construction products are made each year from paper, including insulation, gypsum wallboard, roofing paper, flooring, padding, and sound-absorbing materials.
- Recycling one ton of paper saves seventeen mature trees, 7,000 gallons of water, three cubic yards of landfill space, two barrels of oil, and 4,100 kilowatt-hours of electricity—enough energy to power the average American home for five months.

Metals

- It takes eighty to one hundred years for an aluminum can to decompose (break down) in a landfill.
- About 70% of all metal is used just once and then discarded. The remaining 30% is recycled. After five cycles, one-fourth of 1% of the metal remains in circulation.
- All steel products contain at least 25% steel scrap, which requires 95% less energy to produce than virgin steel and results in an 86% reduction in air pollution and a 76% reduction in water pollution.
- In 2000, approximately 36 billion aluminum cans, having a scrap value of more than $600 million, were landfilled. No wonder scrap metal has become such a valuable commodity.
- More than 50% of an aluminum can is made from recycled aluminum.

Glass

- Glass takes over 1,000,000 (one million) years to decompose in a landfill.
- Glass never wears out. It can be recycled forever! We save over a ton of resources for every ton of glass recycled: 1,330 pounds of sand, 433 pounds of soda ash, 433 pounds of limestone, and 151 pounds of feldspar.
- Most bottles and jars contain at least 25% recycled glass.

Plastics

- It can take up to 700 years for plastic to decompose in a landfill.
- Americans use 25 billion plastic bottles every year. If every American household recycled just one out of every ten HDPE (high density polyethylene) bottles they used, we'd keep 200 million pounds of the plastic out of landfills every year.
- PET plastic can be recycled into clothing, fiberfill for sleeping bags, toys, stuffed animals, rulers, and more.

Rubber (Synthetic)

- It takes half a barrel of crude oil to produce the rubber for just one truck tire.
- Every two weeks, Americans wear almost 50 million pounds of rubber off their tires. That's enough to make 3 1/4 million new tires from scratch.
- Producing one pound of recycled rubber versus one pound of new rubber requires only 29% of the energy.

Reclaimed wood has already made substantial inroads as a replacement material. Close on its heels are brick, steel, and other structural materials that were historically destined for the landfill at the end of what was thought to be their useful lives, but for which sustainable options are now being reintroduced, dramatically extending the useful life of the material while reducing the waste. Hardware and some fixtures can also be reused, either within the structure itself or on other construction projects.

Building rating systems typically offer credits for the reuse of materials, either in a specific category or under the recycled content section. Management of construction waste and demolition debris also provides benefits as the reuse of these materials dramatically cuts down on what is routed to a landfill. Reusing materials and eliminating what ends up in the landfill give you a double play in sustainable materials benefits.

Choosing Rapidly Renewable Materials

Building material selection affect the entire extraction, processing, and transportation network. Manufacturing activities may pollute, deplete, and destroy natural environments. The EPA estimates that building-related construction and demolition debris totals more than 136 million tons a year, or nearly 40% of the entire solid waste stream. You can reduce the use and depletion of finite raw materials and long-cycle renewable materials by replacing them with rapidly renewable materials.

The USGBC defines rapidly renewable materials as natural, non-petroleum-based building materials that have harvest cycles under ten years. Such materials include bamboo, straw, cork, linoleum products, wool, cotton, and bio-based boards such as wheat, sunflower seed hull, and sorghum.

These organic materials are plant or animal-based and can replace the long growth cycle materials such as hardwoods (which can take hundreds of years to grow to a harvestable size) or natural stone (which can take thousands of years to form). The use of materials such as bamboo —which self-generates, grows very quickly, and is formed into sheet goods that can be stronger and more durable than virgin wood alternatives—has created a new material category for bio-based materials. Another example of a rapidly renewable alternative is to replace fiberglass, which can irritate skin when installed as insulation, with cotton or wool—both natural fibers that grow quickly and cleanly, and can be used to more safely and comfortably to insulate walls.

The range of rapidly renewable and bio-based products is limited only by our imagination. Widespread adoption may be slowed by the cost effectiveness of commercial production. Currently, rapidly renewable building materials are more expensive than their synthetic counterparts—linoleum, for example, comes at a premium compared to vinyl flooring.

As interest in green products grows and the benefits of rapidly renewable materials become well understood, the economics of supply and demand will bring the prices of rapidly renewable materials down. Ultimately, rapidly renewable materials will help us produce better buildings with smaller environmental footprints.

Specifying Certified Wood

Wood can be a renewable resource if it is harvested in a sustainable manner. Americans use about 27% of the wood commercially harvested worldwide. Unfortunately, much of it is harvested in an unsustainable way, making the burden on forest ecosystems that much greater. To reduce the burden, our options are, of course, (1) to use less wood, (2) reuse wood that has already been harvested, and/or (3) buy wood that was harvested in a way that minimizes damage to local communities and forest ecosystems.

With forest certification, an independent organization develops standards of good forest management, and independent auditors issue certificates to those forest operations that comply with the standards. Such certification verifies that forests are well-managed (as defined by a particular standard) and ensures that certain wood and paper products come from responsibly managed forests.

There are over fifty wood certification programs worldwide, with four in North America: the American Tree Farm

System (ATFS), the Canadian Standards Association (CSA), the Forestry Stewardship Council (FSC), and the Sustainable Forestry Initiative (SFI) Program. Thus far, the largest and most well-regarded certification program is the one developed by the FSC.

© 1996 Forest Stewardship Council A. C.

The FSC seeks to ensure that wood is harvested in a more responsible fashion. Through third party certifiers, such as Smartwood and Scientific Certification Systems (SCS), FSC certifies that forests are managed in a manner that:

- Supports fair labor policies,
- Respects local influence over forestry operations,
- Protects forest ecosystems (including native species, watersheds, and soils), and
- Avoids the use of chemicals and genetic engineering.[25]

While forest certification is becoming more popular, only a small fraction of the world's forests are certified; the majority of the wood supply is still non-certified. You can encourage environmentally responsible forest management directly by purchasing certified products and indirectly by seeking out reclaimed or recycled alternatives to virgin wood products.

When evaluating forest certification programs, look for:

- A rigorous, science-based standard that covers key values such as protection of biodiversity, species at risk, and wildlife habitat; sustainable harvest levels; protection of water quality; and prompt regeneration.
- Independent, third-party certification audits performed by internationally accredited certification bodies.
- Publicly available certification summary documents with corrective actions listed.
- Transparent standard setting and complaints processes.
- Support from conservation organizations that share similar goals for responsible forest management.

Reducing Carbon

The majority of fuels used worldwide to power industry and society contain carbon. When these fuels are burned to release energy, carbon dioxide and other damaging gases are released into the atmosphere. Fossil fuels take millions of years to create and are being rapidly depleted in an unsustainable manner through transportation uses, manufacturing, and energy consumption. This imbalance has created a need to transition to a more resource-efficient, low-carbon economy. One way to reduce our carbon impact is to buy locally manufactured materials, which reduces transportation-related carbon emissions and helps to stimulate the local economy. Some products, like concrete, steel, gypsum, plywood, MDF, and particle board, are relatively easy to source locally, and contribute significantly to achieving a low carbon footprint.

The U.S. Green Building Council defines local (or regional) materials as those within 500 miles of the project site. To pursue this credit in the LEED system, the materials must be harvested, extracted, and manufactured within 500 miles of the building site. Although it may be substantially cheaper to harvest and manufacture materials in other parts of the world, limiting the transport of materials to within 500 miles of a project site goes a long way in reducing carbon emissions.

For products that are manufactured in the U.S., be sure to discuss with a representative what manufacturing plants their products are coming from. This information will help you to select products from the plant closest to you whenever possible. Also, get to know the folks at your local green building council; they can help you identify locally manufactured products. By using indigenous resources, you are not only reducing the environmental impact from transportation, you are making an important contribution to increasing the demand for building materials and products that are extracted and manufactured within your region and thus to their availability.

Social Impacts

The concept of "corporate social responsibility" is being driven from both ends of the spectrum, corporations and consumers. On one side, a growing group of companies believe that they can both "do-good" and make profits. These companies are seeking to do the right thing, reduce liability, and create positive brand perceptions for their various stakeholders. Unfortunately, these companies do not represent the majority. So, on the other end of the spectrum are consumers who believe that companies are responsible for more than the products they sell and that a company's operations also have a direct impact on the well-being of its employees and the community in which it operates. Subscribers to this belief want manufacturers to take responsibility for safe working conditions, fair pay, equitable opportunities, and to report on and improve their overall impact on the environment. This consumer movement aims to put pressure on companies that are not proactively adopting corporate social responsibility directives.

Among the many issues to consider when purchasing and specifying building materials is the concept of *ethical consumerism* or *socially responsible purchasing*. These terms refer to buyers who favor and support products and businesses that operate on principles benefiting the greater good rather than self-interest or business-interest alone. Ethical or socially responsible consumers are motivated to purchase products that are made without harming or exploiting humans, animals, or the natural environment.

Key social concerns include:

- **Labor practices:** Ensuring the safety, health, and well-being of the workers who produce the products.
- **Fair trade:** Ensuring that producers of raw materials, such as farmers and miners, receive a fair price and are empowered with the knowledge, skills, and resources to improve their businesses, thereby building sustainability in their communities.
- **Corporate transparency:** Seeking transparency in reporting corporate impacts on environment, health, and social justice.

Let's explore each of these in more detail.

Labor Practices

The International Labor Rights Forum describes the crisis of unfair labor practices this way:

Millions of workers around the world toil under inhumane working conditions. In a globalized economy, corporations from developed countries produce consumer goods ranging from coffee to cell phones in poor developing countries, where they can take advantage of cheap labor and lack of environmental or community protections. Workers, including child workers, must toil extremely long hours for wages that are barely subsistence wages, and often under unsanitary and unsafe conditions. In many countries there is little or no labor law enforcement, and many workers are prevented from joining organizations to advance their interests. Alarmingly, an estimated 211 million children between the ages of 5 and 14 are compelled to work around the world. These children produce rubber, clothing, and coffee and work in mines to produce goods that are traded to the U.S. and other developed countries. Unable to go to school, these children face little hope of escaping poverty in their future.[26]

The Bureau of Labor Statistics reports that in the U.S. alone 4,000 to 5,000 workers die from acute on-the-job injuries every year while another 60,000 workers are estimated to die each year from cancer, lung disease, and other chronic illnesses from work-related exposures to hazardous chemicals.[27]

Chemicals and materials embedded in the final product often are present in the manufacturing workplace at elevated concentrations, posing acute or chronic health and safety threats to exposed workers. In most countries, companies have a legal obligation to fully notify workers about such risks and to comply with all regulations protecting worker health and safety.

Many nonprofit and government organizations are working towards safe and equitable labor practices around the world. If you are concerned about sourcing products that uphold fair labor practices, refer to the Scientific Certification

Systems (SCS) for Fair Labor Practices (www.scs-certified.com). While relatively new, companies that source from traditionally disadvantaged regions can use this certification to build consumer confidence and gain marketing advantage. You may also want to check that the product is manufactured in a country that belongs to the International Labor Organization (ILO). The ILO is a United Nations agency that brings together governments, employers, and workers of its member states in common action to promote decent work conditions throughout the world. Currently, 183 countries are members of the ILO (a complete list can be found at www.ilo.org).

Fair Trade

The Fair Trade Federation defines fair trade as

a movement to provide market access to otherwise marginalized producers, connecting them to customers and allowing access with fewer middlemen. It aims to provide higher wages than typically paid to producers as well as helping producers develop knowledge, skills, and resources to improve their lives—thereby building sustainability in their communities. Products are imported and/or distributed by fair trade organizations (commonly referred to as alternative trading organizations) or by "product certification," whereby products complying with fair trade specifications are certified indicating that they have been produced, traded, processed, and packaged in accordance with the standards.[28]

This system of exchange seeks to create greater equity and partnership in the international trading system by:

- Creating opportunities for economically and socially marginalized producers
- Developing transparent and accountable relationships
- Building capacity
- Paying promptly and fairly
- Supporting safe and empowering working conditions
- Ensuring the rights of children
- Cultivating environmental stewardship
- Respecting cultural identity

Fair Trade emerged as an alternative to International Aid in the 1960s in an attempt to create sustainable economies in developing countries. Most fair trade initiatives deal with products that stem from agricultural raw materials, such as coffee, tea, flowers, textiles, and hand-crafted goods. Providers of these materials have often been at the mercy of markets, where prices can fall below costs and producers lack the skills, resources, and power to negotiate a better outcome. When choosing products derived from agricultural sources, seek items that carry labels approved by the Fair Trade Federation.

Corporate Transparency

While we've elected to touch on the topic of corporate transparency here in our discussion of social impacts, we could easily argue that the topic deserves its own section in this book. Our basic knowledge of products, their make-up, manufacturing, and labor practices, etc., all depend on a company's willingness to share accurate information and its commitment to continually improve its products and processes as a result of stakeholder feedback and analytical data.

In the book, *The Triple Bottom Line*, author Andrew Savitz describes the current corporate environment:

> *Call it the age of accountability: corporate leaders that want their companies to survive for the long haul must develop a more integrated, responsible, and sustainable way of doing business—driven not by philanthropy or government regulation but by the hard and fast truths of succeeding in a global economy. They must find ways to provide an array of benefits to the world even as they enrich their shareholders.*[29]

When companies apply "triple bottom-line thinking" to their business practices and accounting, they expand the traditional reporting framework to take into account ecological and social performance, as well as financial. An international non-profit organization, The Global Reporting Initiative (GRI), has created a template and process for reliably communicating this sort of sustainability information. GRI's Sustainability Reporting Framework is gaining credibility across industries and sectors and may emerge as a widely adopted standard. A number of variations have been developed based on the GRI framework; these aim at addressing various business types more specifically, such as small- to medium-sized businesses that are not structured in the same way as larger companies with more resources.[30]

Taking the holistic approach yet one step further, some companies are seeking a reclassification of their corporate status to a "B" corporation, meaning "Beneficial." To explain, a nonprofit organization called B Lab (www.bcorporation.net) is moving state to state to introduce legislation that will allow B-Corporations to exist as legal entities. B Lab is bringing attention to the fact that traditional companies are legally required to *maximize* shareholder profits—indeed, shareholders can hold corporate leaders accountable if they do otherwise. In an effort to maximize profits, companies don't necessarily consider the repercussions.

For example, if a company leader decides that it is more profitable to move manufacturing to China, even though doing so would compromise the well-being of the workers and the community at large, corporate law requires that business leaders do what is best for the shareholders (to maximize profits) versus what is best for the stakeholders. B Lab recognized that many successful companies are both profitable *and* socially responsible, so a B-Corporation could amend its articles of incorporation to include consideration of stakeholders (not just shareholders) such as employees, the surrounding community, and the environment. Until B-Corporations are officially recognized as legal entities, B Lab is certifying them based on compliance with several standards that encompass the environment, philanthropy, diversity, and transparency. B-Corporations' transparent and comprehensive performance standards enable consumers to support businesses that align with their values, investors to drive capital to higher impact investments, and governments and multinational corporations to implement sustainable procurement policies.

While these types of reporting and certification systems are taking hold, look for signs that companies are providing transparency and leadership in reporting. These signs include:

- Full product content disclosure on the product label or in product literature;
- Concern for green chemistry, such as a Cradle-to-Cradle product certification;
- Environmentally-optimized manufacturing processes, such as clean manufacturing technologies, a closed loop water system, and on-site renewable energy;
- Supplier incentives to meet and exceed corporate sustainability practices;
- Auditing and verification programs for overseas supply chain operations;
- Engagment in environmental stewardship, such as land conservancy and protection;
- Commitment to the International Organization for Standardization (ISO) 14001, which addresses various aspects of environmental management and provides guidelines and requirements to uphold; and
- Publication of an annual public corporate sustainability report that includes environmental, health, and social performance.

In the green building industry, people are always asking or looking for the "greenest" or "most sustainable" product. We must understand that the perfect product doesn't exist, and trade-offs will always exist between and among performance, durability, cost, aesthetics, and most recently, sustainability. Perhaps a product is rapidly renewable and sustainably harvested, like bamboo, but comes from China and therefore introduces the concern of carbon in the transportation process or labor practices in a foreign country. The benefits and drawbacks must be weighed against one another when making choices in material selection.

Now that we have offered some background on assessing a product's impact on health, sustainability, and social issues, we'd like to touch on some more specific issues regarding material selection. In the next two chapters, we provide guidelines and tools to help you better evaluate materials and make more appropriate material selections for you and your clients.

Chapter 3: Labels and Certifications

With a multitude of products available all touting sustainable attributes, it can be difficult to determine the "best" material to suit a project's needs. So how do you decide between a product that has a high recycled content and one made of virgin materials that claims to be non-toxic and healthy? And who can be trusted in a field where most of the information come from the manufacturer selling the products?

"Greenwashing" (as mentioned earlier, the practice of companies making marketing claims that spin their products and policies as environmentally friendly when in fact they are not) has increased so dramatically that the Federal Trade Commission (FTC) has updated its *Guides for the Use of Environmental Marketing Claims* to address environmental claims. While the FTC currently requires that every expressed and implied claim regarding a material be substantiated, we cannot rely on them to police the industry and ensure claims are true. We must become educated consumers—able to sort out the greenwashing from the truth.

Many individuals who specify or purchase products may be aware of the environmental attributes they should be looking for, but it's difficult to successfully weigh the legitimate information and competitive priorities of a product in order to make the best decision. Indeed, it can be challenging to make sound decisions on the appropriateness of one material, product, or technology over another.

Several rating systems have emerged with the goal of making sustainable product selection easier; however, they have proliferated so quickly and measure such a plethora of green attributes that some confusion has arisen about how to use these systems effectively. Labels, certifications, and rating systems can help guide both specifiers and consumers looking for green products, but only to the degree that we understand the basis on which the certification is given.

Our aim in this chapter is to demystify the various certifications and rating systems for construction materials so that you can identify those most relevant to you, making your product selection and purchasing process—and ultimately your job—much easier.

Types of Claims

Let's begin by defining a couple of terms. *Certification* means that a product has been evaluated and meets predetermined criteria. A *standard* is a set of guidelines and criteria against which a product can be evaluated. We'll first review product certifications, and then take a look at the standards.

It's important to note that there are varying degrees of credibility in certification programs:

- *First-party:* General marketing claims, product specifications, and material safety data sheets (MSDS) are first-party declarations that a company makes about their own products, but the claims have not been independently tested or verified.
- *Second-party:* By involving a trade association or outside consulting firm in setting standards and verifying claims, second-party claims provide more credible information. Second-party certifications are often industry-driven, so they represent the interest of the industry and may not incorporate or fully consider the best interests of the consumer or society at large.
- *Third-party:* The most credible certification programs are based on a rigorous process that first crafts and

then promulgates the standards. Once the standards have been established, an independent third party tests the materials or products and, if they meet the standards, the third party awards the certification.

Most certifications for green building products are moving toward second- and third-party verifications. Beware of first-party declarations.

Setting Standards

To ensure integrity, a certification should be based on a known standard. Standards ensure desirable characteristics of products and services such as quality, environmental friendliness, safety, reliability, efficiency, and interchangeability.

Setting an industry-wide standard is a formal process that engages a broad range of stakeholders including users, industry experts, scientists and environmentalists, manufacturers, policy makers, and government officials. The process involves convening a technical working group to draft standards, conducting formal reviews, voting, resolving issues, and building consensus for both the specific content of the standard (what it covers and the basis on which compliance will be determined) as well as the specific text that expresses the standard in writing. This process can take many months, even years, but ultimately results in a standard that has credibility and thus greater ability to gain broad acceptance when introduced to the industry. For example, the USGBC used that process to establish the LEED rating system, a process they continue to use as they work on improvements and advances in the system. To further ensure credibility, standards should be available for public review. To provide transparency when standards require lab testing, independent laboratories should be used to ensure impartial data.

The highest level authorities in developing standards are the International Organization for Standardization (ISO) and its American counterpart, the American National Standards Institute (ANSI). ISO is the world's largest developer and publisher of international standards; 162 countries belong to ISO, each with its own standards institute.

Standards ensure desirable characteristics of products and services such as quality, environmental friendliness, safety, reliability, efficiency, and interchangeability—and at an economical cost. ISO standards:

- Make the development, manufacturing, and supply of products and services more efficient, safer, and cleaner;
- Facilitate trade between countries and make it fairer;
- Provide governments with a technical base for health, safety and environmental legislation, and conformity assessment;
- Share technological advances and good management practice;
- Disseminate innovation; and
- Safeguard consumers, and users in general, from products and services.

When products, systems, machinery and devices work well and safely, it is often because they meet standards.

The ANSI is the official U.S. representative to the ISO. ANSI provides accreditation for product certification programs, helping to ensure that the marketplace can gain confidence in the validity of the certification programs and process.

While ANSI is involved in many different industries, its involvement in green building is primarily focused on green building standards, such as the National Green Building Standard that defines green building for residential projects—the basis of the NAHB rating system—and the Green Building Assessment Protocol for commercial building, the basis for the Green Building Initiative's (GBI) Green Globe rating system.

Specifically focusing on social and environmental issues, the ISEAL Alliance is working to establish and improve on standards in the areas of fair trade, forest stewardship, sustainable agriculture, and marine stewardship, among others.

Another body that establishes standards and evaluates compliance is Scientific Certification Systems (SCS). SCS offers several scientific, standards-based product certifications, with both single and multiple attribute certification programs, for green building products. SCS implements a wide range of certification programs. Some of the certifications are developed by independent organizations such as the Forest Stewardship Council Certification (FSC) and the Resilient Floor Covering Institute (RFCI), but SCS also develops its own standards, including those that focus on indoor air quality and recycled content. SCS-certified products include carpet, molding, doors, drywall, office and systems furniture, pest control, paints, insulation, and cleaning products. These certifications share the same standard as LEED requirements. When building rating systems and certifications align—that is, when both are based on the same standard—it helps specifiers more quickly assess whether a product will contribute to the building certification. Here are some examples:

- *level™—Furniture Sustainability* (www.scscertified. com/gbc/level.php)
  Office furniture systems, components, and seating that meet specific criteria within this certification program may contribute to several credits within LEED Version 3.0: Materials and Resources: Credit 4: Recycled Content; Materials and Resources: Credit 6: Rapidly Renewable Materials; Materials and Resources: Credit 7: Certified Wood; and Indoor Environmental Quality: Credit 4.5: Low-Emitting Materials—Systems

Furniture and Seating. Additionally, level-certified products may meet the requirements of the ANSI/BIFMA X7.1-2007 (Low-Emitting Office Furniture Systems and Seating Standard), the California Section 01350 Specification, Collaborative for High Performance Schools (CHPS) Credit EQ 2.2 (Low-emitting Materials), and California Department of General Service (DGS) Indoor Air Quality Specifications for Open Panel Office Furniture (2006).

- *Indoor Advantage* (www.scscertified.com/gbc/ indooradvantage.php)
  Office furniture systems, components, and seating that meet the criteria for this indoor air emissions certification program also meet the criteria of ANSI/BIFMA M-7.1-2007 and ANSI/BIFMA X-7.1-2007 Furniture Emissions Standards, and therefore the criteria for LEED—Commercial Interiors EQ Credit 4.5.

- *Indoor Advantage Gold* (www.scscertified.com/gbc/ indooradvgold.php)
  Building materials such as adhesives and sealants, paints and coatings, textiles and wall coverings, and composite wood, as well as classroom and office furniture systems, components, and seating that earn this SCS certification meet the indoor air emission criteria of California 01350, the California Indoor Air Quality (IAQ) Specifications for Open Panel Office

Furniture, and LEED EQ 4.1, 4.2, 4.4, and 4.5. Certified products may also comply with the Collaborative for High Performance Schools (CHPS) 2009 low-emitting materials requirements.

- *FloorScore (www.scscertified.com/gbc/floorscore.php)*
  A voluntary independent program developed by the Resilient Floor Covering Institute (RFCI), FloorScore is managed by SCS. Hard surface flooring and flooring adhesives that earn this certification also meet the indoor air emission criteria of California 01350 and LEED EQ 4.1 and 4.3.

- *Recycled Material Content (www.scscertified.com/gbc/material_content.php)*
  Products certified by SCS for pre-consumer and/or post-consumer content can help a project qualify for rating system credits such as LEED MR 4.1 and/or LEED MR 4.2.

- *Sustainable Choice (http://www.scscertified.com/gbc/sustainablecarpet.php)*
  Carpets and rugs earning this SCS certification may qualify for LEED EQ 4.3 for low-emitting carpets.

- *CARB ATCM (No Formaldehyde) (www.scscertified.com/gbc/calcompliant.php)*
  In January 2009, the California Air Resources Board (CARB) began enforcing compliance with Phase 1 of the Airborne Toxic Control Measure (ATCM 93120) to control formaldehyde emissions from composite wood products. Compliance requires certification by a CARB-approved third-party certifier (TPC). This applies to composite wood, laminate, and adhesive products. Products certified by SCS either for No Added Urea Formaldehyde or No Added Formaldehyde meet the criteria for LEED EQ 4.4.

- *Forest Stewardship Council (FSC) (http://www.scscertified.com/nrc/fsc_chain_of_custody.php)*
  Companies earning FSC Chain-of-Custody certification from SCS may sell products that qualify for LEED MR 7 Credit.

Evaluating Certification Systems

Before you rely on a certification program, it's a good idea to critically evaluate the following:

- *Certification Based on Standards:* Is the certification based on a standard? As discussed earlier, systems that are certified by national and/or international standard bodies, such as ISO or ANSI, may meet a higher level of quality and consistency. Standards bodies may also provide industry oversight, adding another measure of accountability.

- *Cost of Certification:* How does the cost of certification influence which products seek certification?

With few exceptions, most certifications require manufacturers to pay for certification or inclusion in a directory. This practice, while understandable, can skew databases toward the largest manufacturers and exclude small, innovative manufacturers. For example, the LEED standard for Indoor Environmental Quality incorporates VOC emissions levels and was based on a test protocol widely known as Section 1350, developed by the California Department of Health Services. The alternative test protocol was Greenguard certification. The cost to test a product to determine whether it meets CA 1350 is a few hundred dollars. In contrast, the cost to achieve Greenguard certification runs tens of thousands of dollars. If Greenguard were the only acceptable standard, many organizations simply could not afford to have their products certified due to the prohibitive cost.

- *Green Building Rating System Credit Categories:* Do the relevant rating systems accept the particular certification as verification that a product contributes to green building status? Green building rating systems such as LEED, Green Globes, and NAHB's Standard are creating significant demand for green building products. If these programs accept a certification as verification that a product contributes to a certain category, such acceptance is an indication that the certification has been vetted by them for strengths and weaknesses and has been found to have integrity.

  The reverse is also happening. Many green product certification and labeling systems have emerged to help verify that products contribute to these system credits. While these certifications are often not required to achieve the rating system credits, many specifiers and consumers have become skeptical of manufacturers' marketing claims. As a result, specifiers and buyers are more likely to select a product whose claims have been verified by an objective third party. At this time, most of the certifications accepted by green building rating systems are single attribute certifications.

- *Multiple Levels:* What level of certification is appropriate for your project? Certification systems that have multiple achievement levels can help to further differentiate between the environmental and social impacts of similar products, providing another layer to material selection information. For example, a product that has achieved Cradle to Cradle Silver Certification may be eligible for Gold or Platinum certification, but until a site visit to the manufacturing facility has been completed to verify claims of labor practices, energy use, waste practices, etc., the product cannot achieve the next level of certification. Some product rating systems such as Pharos Lens (www.pharosproject.net)

will inform the manufacturer and publish the steps or documentation needed to achieve a higher level of certification.

- **Third-Party Certification:** Which third-party certifications pertain to the products you're using in your project? Review by an independent and unbiased third party is currently the most reliable method of verifying claims of product "greenness" and "sustainability." Examples of third-party certifications are noted in the following pages.

The rest of this chapter is devoted to a summary of the common and emerging labels and certifications, organized as follows:

- **Single Attribute Certifications:** A simple system based on a single performance attribute, e.g., energy or recycled content.
- **Multiple Attribute Certifications:** Complex assessments that rely on multiple, science-based criteria for determining whether or not a product qualifies to be certified.
- **Life Cycle Assessment (LCA):** A quantitative decision-making tool that analyzes environmental impacts of products and processes over their entire life cycles—

from cradle to grave. Life cycle thinking provides the basis for the multiple attribute product certifications, but life cycle assessment is the ultimate attempt to examine the full range of impacts. This topic will be addressed in detail in Chapter 4.

- **Other (such as Directories):** Listings of available green building products. While there is a nearly endless list of possible certifications for green building products, we have focused on certifications that are U.S.-based and meet the general criteria outlined earlier.

Single Attribute Certifications

The following examples of single attribute certifications cover sustainably harvested wood, VOC levels, energy reductions (compared to average products), and water reduction (compared to average products). These certifications entail relatively straightforward evaluations based on a single performance attribute. Each requires more than just first-party claims; either second- or third-party verification is necessary to receive the certification.

Wood

Wood is a renewable resource if it is harvested in a sustainable manner. With forest certification, an independent organization develops standards of good forest management and independent auditors issue certificates to forest operations that comply with those standards. This certification verifies that forests are well-managed—as defined by a particular standard—and ensures that certain wood and paper products come from responsibly managed forests. Sustainably harvested wood is a single attribute certification; however, most wood certifications are based on a standard that includes multiple attributes, as there is no one way to assess the issue. Looking at wood from a multiple attribute perspective means examining growing practices, water conservation, pesticide, and chemical use, transportation issues, and perhaps even how the wood is used at the end of that useful life.

There are over fifty wood certification programs worldwide. We include three of the most common below.

© 1996 Forest Stewardship Council A. C.

FSC Certified
Forest Stewardship Council
www.fscus.org
The FSC's mission is to promote environmentally appropriate, socially beneficial, and economically viable management of the world's forests. To achieve these ends, the FSC has set forth principles, criteria, and standards that span environmental, social, and economic concerns:

- **Environmentally appropriate** forest management ensures that the harvest of timber and non-timber products maintains the forest's biodiversity, productivity, and ecological processes.
- **Socially beneficial** forest management helps both local people and society at large to enjoy long-term benefits and also provides strong incentives to local people to sustain the forest resources and adhere to long-term management plans.
- **Economically viable** forest management means that forest operations are structured and managed to be sufficiently profitable, without generating financial profit at the expense of the forest resources, the ecosystem or affected communities.

The FSC standards were developed from an array of perspectives regarding what represents a well-managed and sustainable forest. While the discussion continues, the FSC standards for forest management have now been applied in over fifty-seven countries around the world.

FSC accredited, independent, third-party certification bodies or "certifiers" certify forests. They assess forest management using FSC principles, criteria, and standards, although each certifier uses their own evaluative process. This allows FSC to remain outside of the assessment process itself, thus supporting the integrity of the standard and the FSC system. Certifiers evaluate both forest management activities (forest certification) and tracking of forest products (chain-of-custody certification). There are twelve FSC-accredited certifiers around the globe.

Courtesy of SFI, Inc.

SFI Certified

Sustainable Forestry Initiative
www.sfiprogram.org
The Sustainable Forestry Initiative is a nonprofit organization founded by the American Forest and Paper Association (the American timber industry's trade association) to provide a forest certification program. As of January 1, 2007, the SFI program became an independent organization, being governed by an independent board of directors that includes nonprofit environmental groups and forest products companies. SFI relies on independent, third-party audits. The SFI 2010–2014 Standard promotes sustainable forest management, with measures to protect water quality, biodiversity, wildlife habitat, species at risk, and Forests with Exceptional Conservation Value. With approximately 180 million acres certified, SFI is the largest single forest certification standard in the world. SFI has made its current standard more rigorous and now addresses most of the issues in the FSC. FSI has

been generally less prescriptive than FSC and has been criticized by the environmental community for that perceived shortcoming.

Programme for the Endorsement of Forest Certification Schemes

www.pefc.org
A European standard that is gaining international recognition is the PEFC Council. PEFC is an independent, nonprofit, nongovernmental organization founded in 1999 to promote sustainably managed forests through independent, third-party certification. The PEFC provides an assurance mechanism to purchasers of wood and paper products that they are promoting the sustainable management of forests.

Indoor Air Quality (VOC emissions)

As we indicated earlier, unhealthy buildings have significant impacts on the productivity and satisfaction of tenants and present real risks for their owners. Most indoor air pollution comes from sources inside the building. Adhesives, carpeting, upholstery, manufactured wood products, and cleaning agents may emit volatile organic compounds (VOCs). VOCs can cause chronic and acute health problems; some are known carcinogens. The labels described below test for various VOCs. The standard on which each is based is noted in the description.

Floor Score

Scientific Certification Systems

www.scscertified.com

The FloorScore® program, developed by the Resilient Floor Covering Institute (RFCI) in conjunction with Scientific Certification Systems (SCS), tests and certifies flooring products for compliance with indoor air quality emission requirements adopted nationwide. Flooring products include vinyl, polymeric flooring, linoleum, laminate flooring, engineered hardwood flooring, ceramic flooring, and rubber flooring.

A flooring product bearing the FloorScore® seal has been independently certified by SCS to comply with the volatile organic compound emissions criteria of the California Section 01350 standard and has passed a third-party certification process.

Courtesy of the Carpet & Rug Institute.

Green Label Plus

Carpet and Rug Institute

www.carpet-rug.org

This standard was developed by the Carpet and Rug Institute (CRI), a national trade association representing over 90% of the carpet and rug manufacturers and suppliers to the industry. The mission of the organization is "to help members become more profitable and grow—by aggressively advocating for the industry and its products, addressing member-identified barriers."

Green Label and Green Label Plus are second-party certifications, where testing is overseen by independent labs.

Green Seal

Green Seal Organization

www.greenseal.org

Green Seal (GS) is an independent, non-profit organization that promotes the manufacture, sales and use of environmentally responsible products. Green Seal provides third-party certification based on life cycle standards, meets ISO standards for eco-labeling and is ANSI accredited.

Green Seal is widely known for its certification of paints and coatings (GS-11). For example, LEED Version 3.0 for New Construction accepts Green Seal certified products as meeting the requirement for:

- IEQ Credit 4.1: Low-Emitting Materials—Adhesives and Sealants (based on *GS-36: Green Seal Standard for Commercial Adhesives*)
- IEQ Credit 4.2: Low-Emitting Materials Paints and Coatings (based on *GS-11: Green Seal Standard for Paints* and *GC-03: Green Seal Standard for Anti-Corrosive Paints*)

In this sense, Green Seal is a single attribute certification, but it is worth noting that the GS evaluation criteria are based on a life cycle approach to ensure that all significant environmental impacts are considered in the development of a standard, from raw material extraction through manufacturing, use, and disposal.

Other GS standards include:

- Institutional and Industrial Cleaners Standard (GS-37)
- Commercial and Institutional Cleaning Services Standard (GS-42)
- Paints and Coatings Standard Revision (GS-11)
- Lodging Standard (GS-33)
- Restaurant and Food Service Operations Standard (GS-46)

These standards may also apply to different rating systems.

GREENGUARD Indoor Air Quality Certification

GRENGUARD Environmental Institute
www.greenguard.org

The GREENGUARD Environmental Institute aims to protect human health and improve quality of life by enhancing indoor air quality and reducing people's exposure to chemicals and other pollutants. As an ISO accredited, third-party organization, the GREENGUARD Environmental Institute certifies products and materials for low chemical emissions.

Certified products must meet stringent chemical emissions standards based on established criteria from various public health agencies. The GREENGUARD certification process includes manufacturing facility reviews and site visits; third-party laboratory testing and data analysis; and quarterly monitoring and annual retesting to ensure that products continue to comply with GREENGUARD standards.

GREENGUARD certification is accepted as verification of low-emitting products by sustainable building programs including NAHB, LEED, Green Globes, and others.

This certification is unique in that it goes beyond third-party verification and seeks to be recognized as a third-party endorsement of products, essentially attempting to establish GREENGUARD as the authority amidst the maze of green marketing claims. This effort requires extensive marketing of the GREENGUARD brand to develop awareness in the marketplace, as well as marketing support and message development for manufacturers participating in the GREENGUARD certification programs. These services come at a cost to manufacturers and are reflected in the fees to participate, which are considerably higher than third-party tests that simply certify low-emitting materials.[31]

Energy

The most common labels related to energy involve two very different types of energy issues. Energy Star rates appliances and consumer goods that provide above average performance in energy reduction. Green-e Energy certifies renewable energy sources as being authentic and truly sustainable.

Energy Star

U.S. Environmental Protection Agency
www.energystar.gov
Energy Star, a joint program of the U.S. Environmental Protection Agency and the U.S. Department of Energy, helps protect the environment through energy-efficient products and practices.

Products: Devices carrying the Energy Star logo, such as computer products and peripherals, kitchen appliances, buildings, and other products, generally use 20%–30% less energy than required by federal standards.

Buildings: New homes, buildings, and industrial facilities that meet strict guidelines for energy efficiency can qualify for Energy Star certification. An Energy Star qualified home uses at least 15% less energy than standard homes built to the 2004 International Residential Code (IRC). Energy Star rated homes usually include properly installed insulation, high performance windows, tight construction and ducts, energy-efficient cooling and heating systems, and Energy Star qualified appliances, lighting, and water heaters.

Green-e Energy

www.green-e.org
Developed in conjunction with leading environmental, energy, and policy organizations, Green-e Energy is a second-party certification program for renewable energy that meets environmental and consumer protection standards. The program requires that sellers of certified renewable energy disclose clear and useful information to potential customers, allowing consumers to make informed choices.

Green-e Energy requires organizations offering a certified renewable energy option to:

- Meet the requirements for renewable resources detailed in the Green-e Energy Standard;
- Abide by a professional code of conduct that governs the marketing and business practices of the participating organizations;
- Follow the Green-e Energy Customer Disclosure Requirements, including the following:

- Provide customers with a Product Content Label for the certified renewable energy option, identifying the renewable resource type (such as wind or solar) they supply and the geographic location of the renewable energy generator; and
- Provide customers with simple, clear price, terms, and conditions for the renewable energy option;
- Undergo an annual verification process audit to ensure that they are buying enough of the right types of renewable energy to match their certified sales to customers;
- Complete a twice-annual review of marketing materials to ensure the organization is not making false or misleading statements about its certified renewable energy option(s) and is following the Green-e Energy Customer Disclosure Requirements;
- Pay an annual fee to cover the costs associated with certification.

Water

At this time, there is one primary label that reviews water conservation in consumer products. The WaterSense label is similar to the Energy Star program in that a product receives the label if it outperforms average products.

WaterSense®

A voluntary partnership program sponsored by the U.S. EPA
hwww.epa.gov/WaterSense/
The WaterSense label identifies water-efficient products that are independently tested and certified to meet EPA's criteria. WaterSense also recognizes some professional certification programs that meet WaterSense specifications by incorporating a strong water efficiency component. Products bearing the WaterSense label:

- Perform as well or better than their less efficient counterparts.
- Are about 20% more water-efficient than standard models.
- Realize water savings on a national level.
- Provide measurable water savings results.
- Achieve water efficiency through several technology options.
- Are effectively differentiated by the WaterSense label.
- Are independently certified.

Multiple Attribute Certifications

Multiple attribute certifications look at a product's performance on various measures of sustainability. Each of the certification programs described below goes beyond first-party claims, requiring either second- or third-party verification to achieve certification.

Cradle to Cradle
McDonough Braungart Design Chemistry
www.mbdc.com

Cradle to Cradle Certification provides a company with a means to tangibly, credibly measure achievement in environmentally intelligent design and helps customers purchase and specify products that are pursuing a broader definition of quality. This means the use of environmentally safe and healthy materials; design for material reutilization, such as recycling or composting; the use of renewable energy and energy efficiency, efficient use of water, and maximum water quality associated with production; and instituting strategies for social responsibility.

If a candidate product achieves the necessary criteria, it is certified as a Basic, Silver, Gold, or Platinum product and can be branded as Cradle to Cradle Certified^{CM}.

Cradle to Cradle Certified^{CM} is a certification mark of MBDC, exclusively licensed to the Cradle to Cradle Products Innovation Institute™.

SMART Sustainable Product Standard
The Institute for Market Transformation to Sustainability (MTS)
www.mts.sustainableproducts.com

MTS is a nonprofit public collaboration of leading environmental groups, governments, and companies and is an ANSI Accredited Standards Developer. They have developed SMART Certification for building products, fabric, apparel, textiles, and floor coverings based on environmental, social, and economic criteria. Products can achieve varying levels of certification including Sustainable, Silver, Gold, and Platinum.

SMART represents an effort to consolidate the eco labeling industry and reduce redundancy. MTS adopted the following existing standards and wrapped them up into one certification program:

- FSC Certified Wood
- Greenguard / California 1350 VOC
- LEED
- Green-e Power
- Certified Organic
- GRI Social Equity Indicators
- EPA/Purdue University Best Management Practices
- ISO 14025 LCA
- FTC Environmental Marketing Guides
- Stockholm Treaty Chemical Ban
- State of Minnesota Design for Environment (DfE) Toolkit
- EPA Lifecycle Design

- EPA Environmentally Preferable Product Guidance
- EPA Toxic Release Inventory
- EPA Tool for the Reduction and Assessment of Chemical and other Environmental Impacts (TRACI)
- EPA Closed Loop Process Regulation
- Cleaner and Greener Certification
- Minnesota Public Utilities Commission Cleaner Fuels Spec
- EcoSmart CO_2 Reductions for Concrete and Cement
- ISO 14001 Environmental Management System Environmental Policy and Publicly Available Targets

All certified products must either have an ISO-compliant LCA or actual environmental data on twelve impacts from their suppliers. This is critical because many manufacturers have thousands of suppliers with major environmental impacts. This LCA requirement satisfies almost 60% of available credits for certification.

Uniquely, SMART requirements eliminate key toxic pollutants and provide more credit for those products which contain no toxic endocrine disruptors.

In 2007, through a LEED Credit Interpretation Request (CIR), a building that incorporated more than 2.5% of SMART-certified products (as a percentage of total material costs) would qualify for an Innovation Design point.

The Global Reporting Initiative

www.globalreporting.org

The Global Reporting Initiative (GRI) has emerged as the standard for organizations that report on sustainability. GRI's Sustainability Reporting Framework includes economic, environmental, and social performance in the areas of labor practices and decent work, human rights, impact on society, and product responsibility. GRI's Guidelines outline core content for reporting and are relevant to all organizations regardless of size, sector, or location. The GRI Reporting Framework allows organizations to plot a path for continual improvement of their sustainability reporting practices.

The Reporting Framework also dovetail with the efforts of organizations to provide triple bottom line reporting. This may one day become as routine as current practices in financial reporting.

The Pharos Project

Healthy Building Network

www.pharosproject.net

The Pharos Project seeks to define a consumer-driven vision of truly green building materials and to establish a method for evaluation that is in harmony with principles of environmental health and justice. The Pharos Project is not a product certification system, but rather an online database of building products which are rated in each of sixteen attributes. These ratings are presented in a range that allows users to evaluate which attributes matter most to them/to their project and determine trade-offs for the various environmental, health, and social considerations. The Pharos attributes are grouped into three general areas of concern:

- *Health and Pollution.* Building materials are associated with health impacts on occupants, the fence line communities near the supply chain of the manufacturing process, and the global community. Healthy building products avoid use of materials that cause health and environmental damage from cancer to global warming; damage from resource extraction, refinement, and production; and damage from their use as well as end-of-life handling.
- *Environment and Resources.* Every stage of a product's fabrication expends resources and yields waste. Green product design reduces energy and water use for in manufacturing and ongoing operation of building products; maximizes the use of renewable energy; reduces waste and habitat destruction; and

sets up closed-loop material cycles to infinitely recycle materials into new products.
- *Social and Community.* The Pharos Project supports the idea that a company is responsible for more than the products it sells. A company's operations impact the well-being of its employees and the community in which it operates. Manufacturers have a responsibility to ensure safe working conditions with fair pay and equitable opportunities, to actively engage with and support the local community, and to report on and improve their overall corporate impact.

In the works for several years, The Pharos Project was officially launched at USGBC's Greenbuild Conference and Expo in Phoenix, Arizona, in November 2009. The initial launch includes four of the sixteen attributes rated that cover toxicity and health issues at different stages of production and use. One hundred products have been rated; one hundred more are in the pipeline. The next phase will address attributes related to the social issues of sustainability—an area that no other system is currently addressing.

While this tool will take years to be fully realized, it is on target to be the most comprehensive, transparent, and democratic tool available to manufacturers and users alike.

Pharos does not charge manufacturers to participate. In addition, they provide feedback to manufacturers at no cost, enabling manufacturers to obtain the information they need to continually improve their processes.

Not all sustainable products will have certifications. Many products will make green claims, yet not be truly sustainable. At this time, no single source or label exists on which to rely. However, the industry is moving toward consolidation and verification of certifications that will increase credibility and strengthen consumer confidence.

Directories

The directories listed below contain many sustainable products in a range of categories. These resources can help you find interesting alternatives. Nevertheless, we recommend that you remain vigilant during your search and verify any claims being made. Just because materials are included in a directory does not mean that they have been certified or approved.

GreenSpec

www.buildinggreen.com/menus/index.cfm
Owner: BuildingGreen, LLC
Independent assessments of over 2,000 products that represent the top 10% of green building products

SCS Certified Products Database

www.scscertified.com/ecoproducts/products
Owner: Scientific Certification Systems (SCS)
Searchable listings for all SCS-certified products

AIA Marketplace

info.aia.org/aia/newproductmarketplace.cfm
Owner: American Institute of Architects (AIA)
Includes all types of building products, some of which are green

ARCAT

www.arcat.com/divs/building_products.shtml
Owner: ARCAT
Building products including specifications, SpecWizard, and CAD Details, with green products designated

GreenFormat

www.greenformat.com
Owner: Construction Specifications Institute
General and life cycle product and company information by MasterFormat category

ecoScorecard

www.ecoscorecard.com
Owner: ecoScorecard
Lists the environmental and LEED applicability of green building products from a small but growing group of manufacturers

Low Impact Living

www.lowimpactliving.com/products-providers
Owner: Low Impact Living
Green building products and services

Oikos

www.oikos.com/green_products
Owner: Iris Communications, Inc.
Green products by category and company

Rate It Green

www.rateitgreen.com
Owner: Rate It Green
User-driven green product listings and assessments

CleanGredients

www.cleangredients.org
Owner: GreenBlue
Showcase of potentially harmful ingredients; reviewed by National Sanitation Foundation

Good To Be Green

www.goodtobegreen.com
Owner: Good to be Green
Commercial and residential green building products

Green2Green

www.green2green.org
Owner: GreenBlue
Land, foundation, and insulation green products

Summary

As green building continues to infuse the industry and dominate new construction projects, the product choices will continue to expand and sustainable attributes will grow accordingly. Finding the most appropriate products is a difficult task and one that should be undertaken with the goal of achieving credible results from a valid assessment.

While there are many options available for most products, it is important that specifiers, architects, and consumers themselves have a critical eye when evaluating claims made about products. It is important to understand how to separate a marketing claim from a third-party–verified claim that is based on a reputable standards organization.

Various achievement levels within a standard, such as Gold, Silver, and Bronze, further allow you to differentiate between products in a single category. The various levels help you to determine which manufacturers have pushed their products further along the sustainability curve.

While certifications and standards are beneficial, it is still the user's responsibility to assess which characteristics are most appropriate for their project. It may be more important to your project to have a low-VOC finish on a product than it is to have a product that includes recycled content, especially if

the space is being designed for a chemically sensitive population. End project needs are a crucial factor not only when you
initially assess your material requirements, but also as you write
specifications.

Industry organizations and standards are subject to ongoing change as new products are introduced, new criteria are
established, and results gathered post-installation are incorporated. As you assess products for each project, be sure that you
are referencing the most recent standards.

Chapter 4: Life Cycle Assessment

Environmental product declarations in the form of labels and certifications have proliferated, this we know. These labels and certifications mainly cover what ISO defines as Type I declarations (a seal of approval for meeting a multiple attribute set of predetermined requirements) and Type II declarations (verifiable, single attribute, environmental claims that are either self-declared or verified by a third party).

Single attribute declarations are a step towards understanding the impact of products on the environment and our health, but can be misleading because they ignore the possibility that other life cycle stages, or other environmental conditions, may have an impact as well. For example, a product that is certified to have a high percentage of recycled content is good in that fewer earth-depleting raw materials were used to manufacture it. However, if that recycled content is composed of certain plastics, the chemicals used to break down the plastic so that it could be recycled may cause more harm to the environment than simply using raw materials.

Single attribute certifications lack comprehensive information about the total impact of a product from raw material procurement through the end of its life. If we really want to explore the environmental impacts of a product, we need to investigate all stages of the product's life from beginning to end. This is where life cycle assessment comes in. LCA provides the comprehensive data that consumers and specifiers need to make informed decisions about the holistic impact of products. Such analysis is not easy to do, but recent attention to the subject has led to several initiatives and tools that are helping the industry move closer to more thoroughly adopting life cycle thinking.

A number of methodologies are available for conducting LCA. Our purpose in this chapter is simply to establish a basic framework for the concepts of LCA and how the process of LCA is evolving.

We'll begin by defining LCA, then break down the components and steps, discuss the interpretation of results, and outline the emerging tools to help you evaluate the life cycle of a product. Ultimately, we will give you some simple steps to advance life cycle thinking in your own work.

A Brief History of LCA

While initial LCA-type studies started as early as the 1960s, it wasn't until the 1990s that standards began to emerge. In 1991, concerns over the inappropriate use of LCAs by product manufacturers making broad marketing claims resulted in a statement issued by eleven State Attorneys General in the U.S. denouncing the use of LCA results to promote products until uniform methods for conducting such assessments were developed and a consensus reached on how this type of environmental comparison could be advertised non-deceptively. This action, along with pressure from other environmental organizations to standardize LCA methodology, led to the development of the LCA standards in the International Standards Organization (ISO) 14000 series.

In 2002, the United Nations Environment Programme (UNEP) joined forces with the Society of Environmental Toxicology and Chemistry (SETAC) to launch the Life Cycle Initiative, an international partnership. The three programs of the Initiative aimed at putting life cycle thinking into practice and improving its tools with better data and indicators. The three programs include:

- The Life Cycle Management (LCM) Program creates awareness and improves skills of decision-makers by publishing informative materials, establishing forums for sharing best practice, and carrying out training programs in all parts of the world.
- The Life Cycle Inventory (LCI) Program improves global access to transparent, high quality, life cycle data by hosting and facilitating expert groups whose work results in web-based information systems.
- The Life Cycle Impact Assessment (LCIA) Program increases the quality and global reach of life cycle indicators by promoting the exchange of views among experts whose work results in a set of widely accepted recommendations.

Life Cycle Assessment Defined

Life cycle assessment is a multidisciplinary, scientific approach to investigating and evaluating the environmental impact of a given product or service. All inputs and outputs, such as energy and waste, are considered for each and every phase of the life cycle. Global and regional impacts are calculated based on energy consumption, waste generation, and other criteria.

Some aspects of LCA are being piloted in the LEED system and are utilized in Green Globes; LCA is not currently part of the NAHB rating systems.

LCA is about quantifying and analyzing a product's burdens and impacts from an environmental perspective and should not be confused with Life Cycle Costing (LCC). LCC is strictly a financial tool for calculating the total cost of ownership over the useful life of an asset. Make no mistake, costing information can be useful. Even the most environmentally conscious designer will ultimately weigh environmental benefits against economic costs. When LCA data is factored in along with other data (such as economic value, product performance, durability, etc.), better product choices—those that meet the project requirements *and* have the least impact on the environment—can be made.

So where do you begin? The term *life cycle* refers to the major activities in the course of the product's lifespan, starting with the gathering of raw material from the earth, through the product's manufacture, use, and maintenance, and ending when all materials are returned to the earth at its final disposal. LCA evaluates all of these stages of a product's life, providing a comprehensive view of the environmental aspects of the product or process and a more accurate picture of the environmental trade-offs in product and process selection. LCA is a Type III label (as defined by ISO), which means that it displays comprehensive and detailed product information and is the most in-depth type of label defined by ISO.

Let's now take a look at the six stages in the life cycle of a building material (follow the diagram clockwise).

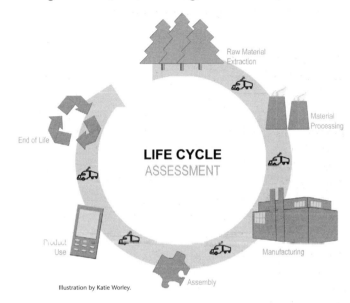

Illustration by Katie Worley.

1. Mining, Extraction, Harvesting
2. Material Processing
3. Manufacturing
4. Assembly
5. Use
6. Disposal and/or Recycling

Within these stages, LCA analyzes the energy, water, waste, and other outputs that may be associated with each stage of a product's life. For most building materials, the major environmental impacts occur during the first two stages of the life cycle. However, as waste disposal issues become more prominent, industries are also being made increasingly aware of the impacts associated with the demolition and disposal stages.

Assessed damages typically fall within one of these common categories: global warming (greenhouse gases), acidification, smog, ozone layer depletion, eutrophication, eco-toxicological and human-toxicological pollutants, habitat destruction, desertification, land use, and the depletion of minerals and fossil fuels.

A life cycle assessment can either be "cradle to cradle" or "cradle to grave." Cradle to grave assumes that the product will end up in a landfill and assesses the environmental impact of that process through those stages. Cradle to cradle assumes that either a portion, or all, of the product can be reused or recycled at the end of its useful life by being reused, upcycled, downcycled, or recycled (as described in Chapter 2).

LCA is not just used on existing products to gain more insight into their lifetime behavior; it is a process that can also be used during the design phase to optimize the environmental performance of a new product before it is introduced to the market. This is known as Eco Design, where the environmental impacts of raw materials, procurement, manufacturing, use, and disposal are primary considerations of the initial design plan.

When used to its fullest potential, the LCA process will be an integral part of designing new products, assessing existing products, and providing feedback for the continual improvement of products towards the lowest environmental impacts.

Life Cycle Methodology

Because it's inherently multidisciplinary, life cycle assessment involves collaboration among a variety of professionals: economists, environmentalists, scientists, standards committees, laboratory technicians, and mathematicians. The quantitative analysis includes measurement, calculations, conversions, and ultimately, data sets. The data must be accurate and clean, as a life cycle assessment is only as valid as the data behind it.

The general LCA methodology involves four steps.[32]

(1) Goal and Scope Definition

Outlining the purpose of the study and its breadth and depth.

One common goal of an LCA is to generate environmental performance scores for product alternatives, but this goal may vary depending on the purpose of the analysis. The scope may outline a few specific environmental impacts that will be examined or it might include a broad array of impacts.

No matter what the goal or scope, it is important in this phase to focus on the stages of the process that will have the greatest impact all the way through the analysis. For example, a single chemical could include more than one hundred flows—elements coming into and going out of the product. By restricting the scope of the analysis to data collection for the specific flows that are actually needed in the subsequent impact assessment, a more focused, higher quality LCA can be conducted. In the strictest sense, an LCA would include an assessment of each and every aspect of the product. By limiting its scope, the LCA process becomes more manageable. For example, scope definition may limit the analysis to the most common environmental impacts.

(2) Inventory Analysis
Identify and quantify the environmental inputs and outputs associated with a product over its entire life cycle. Inputs include water, energy, land, and other resources; outputs include releases to air, land, and water.

In this phase, all of the energy, water, and materials used, as well as all environmental releases (e.g., air emissions, solid waste disposal, wastewater discharges) are identified and quantified. Data categories are used to group these inventory flows. Generally, there are three types of flows in an LCA:

- Elementary flows (emissions or resources), which are emitted into the environment or extracted from it;
- Product flows (goods, services); and
- Waste flows.

A number of approaches may be used to collect inventory data for LCAs, depending on how specific or generalized the data needs to be to accomplish the target scope of analysis. Types of data collection include[33]:

- *Unit Process- and Facility-Specific:* Collects data from a particular process within a given facility. This data collection process does not combine various aspects or various facilities; it is specific to a segment of the product or process.
- *Composite:* Collects data from the same process combined across locations. In this collection process, an average or standard can be established from multiple data points.
- *Aggregated:* Collects data combining more than one

process in the flow. For example, rather than looking at a flow solely for the extraction of ore that will be used in a given product, data for both the extraction of the ore and its transportation to the manufacturing facility could be combined to arrive at an aggregated impact for the use of ore in a product.
- *Industry Average:* Collects data from a representative sample of locations believed to statistically describe the typical process across technologies.
- *Descriptive:* Collects data that may be averaged or based on dispersion but which are qualitatively descriptive of a process.

Publicly available tools such as the Athena Impact Estimator and the Life Cycle Inventory Database by the National Renewable Energy Laboratory (LCI) are being developed to generate average results for generic products, such as a 2x4, from standard data. Through this type of data generalization, which groups similar products together for comparison, an industry average can be established. Once this baseline industry data is established, manufacturers will begin to commission their own LCAs to demonstrate how their products meet or exceed LCA industry standards. Once manufacturer-specific product data is available, unit process- and facility-specific data can be aggregated for use while preserving individual manufacturer confidentiality. The aggregated data can be used in a larger database. For example, the U.S. Life Cycle Inventory Database project began in 2001, when the U.S. Department of Energy (DOE) directed the National Renewable Energy Laboratory (NREL) and the Athena Institute to explore the development of a national public database. The U.S. LCI Database was created and has been publicly available—at www.nrel.gov/lci—since 2003. The goals of the project include:

- Maintain data quality and transparency.
- Cover commonly used materials, products, and processes in the U.S. with up-to-date, critically reviewed LCI data.
- Support the expanded use of LCA as an environmental decision-making tool.
- Maintain compatibility with international LCI databases.
- Provide exceptional data accessibility.
- Support U.S. industry competitiveness.

(3) Impact Assessment

Examines the consequences or impacts of the product on the environment (such as global warming potential).

Moving from flow inventories to the environmental impacts of each of those flows is the most challenging aspect of LCA. This process, known as life cycle impact assessment, is an evolving science based on assumptions and extrapolations from the work of scientists in many fields. The purpose of this phase is to assess the potential human and ecological effects of energy, water, and material usage and the environmental releases identified in the inventory analysis.

Impacts are categorized into a series of common groups called impact categories. The U.S. EPA Office of Research and Development has developed TRACI (Tool for the Reduction and Assessment of Chemical and other environmental Impacts), a set of state-of-the-art, peer-reviewed, U.S. life cycle impact assessment methods that has been adopted by several organizations including LEED Version 3.0 and the BEES LCA tool (which will be described in more detail at the end of this chapter).[34] This model includes impact categories such as Global Warming Potential, Acidification Potential, Eutrophication Potential, Fossil Fuel Depletion, Habitat Alteration, Criteria Air Pollutants, Human Health, Smog, Ozone Depletion, Ecological Toxicity, Water Intake, and Indoor Air Quality.

Several LCA impact assessment approaches attempt to quantify environmental impact. Some focus on a complete chain of impacts;[35] others compare impacts to "ideal" or "target" levels in the environment[36] or try to assess damage to the environment and human health.[37] It will take decades and improved technology to assess *actual* damage. Therefore, to streamline this phase of the LCA, many professionals are focusing on impact indicators that measure *the potential for the impact* to occur rather than directly quantifying actual impacts. While this approach can only project possible impacts, it does work well to simplify the LCA process, making it a more useful tool.

The next step is normalization. Once impacts have been characterized, the resulting impact category performance measures are expressed in units that vary from category to category. For example, global warming is expressed in carbon dioxide equivalents, acidification in hydrogen ion equivalents, eutrophication in nitrogen equivalents, and so on. In order to assist in the next LCA step (*interpretation*), performance measures are often normalized so that they can be placed on the same scale to facilitate the assessment. This normalization of data is necessary to create a level playing field and to gain a better understanding of the relative size of an effect. Each effect calculated for the life cycle of a product is benchmarked against the known total effect for its class. For example, the amount of CO_2 could be normalized with effects caused by the average American during a year. Often expressed in a bar graph, normalization enables the interpreter to see the relative contribution from the material production to each existing effect.

Normalization considerably improves insight into the results, making comparisons a little easier to understand. However, a final judgment cannot yet be made since not all effects are considered to be of equal importance. The final step in the impact assessment is to assign a weight to each of the various impact categories. For example, in the realm of personal health, a bout with acne or dental tartar is not given the same weight as, say, cancer; they are not of equal importance. Similarly, in the evaluation phase, the normalized effect scores are multiplied by a weighting factor representing the relative importance of the effect. Weightings vary greatly between countries, political parties, and scientists. In some of the emerging LCA tools, the user is allowed to choose the weightings or adopt the weighting of various advisory groups.

The current system for assessing impacts is far from perfect. Many known impacts still lack data to accurately calculate the damage to the environment. As yet, there is no generally accepted way of assessing the value of the damage to the environment or ecosystem, if indeed the damage can even be calculated. International databases are currently under development to improve the quality of data for these types of assessments.

(4) Interpretation

Combine the results of the inventory analysis and impact assessment to generate an environmental impact output that can be used to compare products.

Having been put into comparable terms, the normalized impact assessment results can be properly evaluated in the LCA interpretation step. Comparing apples to apples enables users to select the preferred product with a clear understanding of both the assumptions and the uncertainties inherent in generating the results. Generally, a really clear winner or loser among products in the same category is hard to ascertain. Instead, you will gain the most value from this process if you assess the differences in the impacts of the various products you are considering. One product may outperform the competition relative to fossil fuel depletion and habitat alteration, fall short relative to global warming and acidification, and fall somewhere in the middle when it comes to indoor air quality and eutrophication. Take the time to dig in to the individual impacts to determine what matters most with respect to your environmental goals.

It is best to avoid tools that try to reduce LCA results into a single score. The weighting required to achieve a single score relies heavily on assumptions that can guide the user away from a significant understanding of the full environmental and health impacts. These extreme generalizations, or significant rounding of numbers, can lead to material decisions that do not actually reflect the user's environmental goals. Instead, look across the impact categories and make your own assessment based on what matters most to you or your client.

Benefits of LCA

The strength of an environmental LCA is its comprehensive, multi-dimensional scope. The benefit of the LCA approach is that it enables you to conduct a trade-off analysis and thus achieve a genuine reduction in overall environmental impact, rather than a simple shift of impact. By performing an LCA on potential materials, designers and specifiers can:

- Develop a systematic evaluation of the environmental consequences associated with a given product.
- Analyze the environmental trade-offs associated with one or more specific products or processes to help gain stakeholder acceptance.
- Quantify environmental releases to air, water, and land in relation to each life cycle stage.
- Assist in identifying significant shifts in environmental impacts between life cycle stages and environmental media.
- Assess the human and ecological effects of material consumption and environmental releases on the local community, region, and world.
- Compare the health and ecological impacts between two or more rival products/processes or identify the impacts of a specific product or process.
- Identify impacts to one or more specific areas of environmental concern.

A Word of Caution About LCAs

Performing an LCA can be both resource- and time-intensive. Depending on how thorough an LCA is desired, gathering the necessary data can be tricky and the availability of data can greatly affect the accuracy of the final results. Therefore, it is important to weigh the availability of data, the time necessary to conduct the study, and the financial resources required against the projected benefits of the LCA.

LCAs will not determine which product or process is the most cost-effective or performs the best. Therefore, the information developed in an LCA study should be used as one component of a more comprehensive decision-making process assessing the tradeoffs against cost and performance.

As mentioned earlier, an LCA can help identify potential environmental tradeoffs. However, converting the impact results to a single score requires the use of value judgments, which may or may not reflect the user's end goals.

Emerging Tools

Some promising tools are already available to help streamline LCAs, which will no doubt continue to strengthen as resources. Others may emerge over time as well. Existing tools that will help consumers and specifiers conduct their own analyses, evaluation, and decision-making include:

- The Athena Institute's Impact Estimator (assesses whole buildings) and EcoCalculator (assesses building assemblies, especially in relation to rating systems).
- The National Institute of Standards and Technology's (NIST's) Building for Environmental and Economic

Sustainability (BEES) software compares specific products.

No one tool is more prominent or appropriate for every need. If you are looking at assessing building assemblies, your best choice is to use the Athena® EcoCalculator. For whole buildings, consider the Athena® Impact Estimator. If you want to compare various products for inclusion in your design, look at BEES.

Courtesy of the Athena Sustainable Materials Institute. Athena® is a registered trademark of the Athena Sustainable Materials Institute.

The Athena Institute's Impact Estimator and EcoCalculator

The Athena Institute is a nonprofit organization that seeks to improve the sustainability of the built environment by meeting the building community's needs for better information and tools. With offices in Canada and the U.S., the Institute furthers the use and science of LCA through software development, database development, and collaboration with the international research community.

Athena has developed two LCA tools for use in North America—the Athena Impact Estimator for Buildings and the Athena EcoCalculator for Assemblies—both of which focus on whole buildings and assemblies. According to the Athena Institute, the Athena Impact Estimator for Buildings is capable of modeling 95% of the building stock in North America, including industrial, institutional, office, and residential designs (it can be downloaded for a licensing fee at www.athenasmi.org/tools/impactEstimator/order.html). The Athena EcoCalculator for Assemblies (available free of charge at www.athenasmi.org/tools/ecoCalculator/index.html) provides LCA results for common building assemblies based on detailed assessments previously conducted using the Impact Estimator. The spreadsheet tool provides LCA results for hundreds of common building assemblies in low- and high-rise commercial categories, including exterior walls, roofs, intermediate floors, interior walls, windows, and columns and beams. In addition, a new residential version has been developed for single family, duplex, and row houses. The EcoCalculator was originally commissioned by the Green Building Initiative (GBI) for use with the Green Globes environmental assessment and rating system and has been adopted by the USGBC for use in the LEED rating system.

In addition to these tools for LCA, The Athena Institute is also building LCA databases. Recognizing that the quality of the underlying data is essential to establishing a reliable, effective software tool, one of Athena's main thrusts has been the development of comprehensive, comparable databases for building materials and products. Athena's LCA databases cover 95% of the structural and envelope systems typically used in residential and commercial buildings. The Athena Institute also maintains databases for resource use and emissions for onsite construction of a building's assemblies; for maintenance, repair, and replacement effects through the building's operating life; and, at the end of its useful life, for demolition and disposal. The Athena Institute is transparent with its data and makes reports publicly available.

Building for Environmental and Economic Sustainability (BEES)

The U.S. National Institute of Standards and Technology (NIST) Healthy and Sustainable Buildings Program launched the BEES project in 1994. The purpose of BEES was to develop and implement a systematic methodology for selecting building products that provide the most appropriate balance between environmental and economic performance, based on the decision maker's values, and thereby achieving cost-effective reductions in building-related contributions to environmental problems. In addition to generating environmental performance scores for building products in the U.S., BEES LCAs also provide economic performance scores to help the building community select cost-effective, environmentally-preferred building products.

The BEES methodology measures environmental performance using an LCA approach, following guidance from the ISO 14040 standard for LCA.[38] Economic performance is measured separately using the ASTM International standard life cycle cost (LCC) approach.[39] These two performance measures are then synthesized into an overall performance measure using the ASTM standard for Multi-Attribute Decision Analysis.[40] For the entire BEES analysis, building products are defined and classified based on ASTM standard classification for building elements,[41] demonstrating a rigorous and credible basis for the analysis.

In 2007, collaboration between the National Institute for Standards and Technology (NIST) and the Environmental Protection Agency launched BEES 4.0, a Windows-based decision support software program aimed at designers, builders, and product manufacturers. By 2009, the Green Globes rating system and the USGBC's LEED program had begun to incorporate BEES LCA.

BEES LCA software is publicly available, free of charge, and can be downloaded from the NIST site. This powerful, decision-support software is accompanied by a comprehensive, 300+ page manual, an excellent resource in itself. Both are available at www.bfrl.nist.gov/oae/software/bees/.

Life Cycle and Green Building Rating Systems

As we mentioned, LCA is starting to make its way into the forefront of green building rating systems. LCA is utilized in the Green Globes rating system and, in 2009, was incorporated into LEED. To help you understand the future of LCA in green building rating systems, let's review the process the USGBC is using to begin incorporating LCA into their LEED system.

USGBC began by assembling a working group in 2006 tasked with examining the viability of including life cycle assessment in the LEED program. The group's initial recommendation focused on the LCA of assemblies that constitute a building's structure and envelope.

While USGBC has long recognized the value of incorporating LCA-based credits into the LEED rating system, they also realize that the lack of a comprehensive database of building materials, associated data, and an easy user interface will likely slow adoption of LCA for the immediate future. These points notwithstanding, USGBC has stated that any LCA-based LEED credit must meet two essential requirements[42]:

(1) *Level Playing Field:* The LCA basis for any of the proposed LEED credits must provide a level playing field—one that is fair and objective—based on a consistent methodology applied across all products and at all stages of their production, transport, use, and disposal or recycling at end of life.

(2) *Practical Use:* LCA is inherently complex. LCA tools and methods used for LCA-based LEED credits must be very practical as well as intuitively usable

by designers, specifiers, and facilities managers at appropriate stages in the life cycle of buildings.

In October 2009, the USGBC issued six pilot credits including a pilot credit for LCA of Structure and Envelope Assemblies. The intent of these credits was to encourage the use of environmentally preferable building materials and assemblies. While (as of publication of this book) an LCA approach is being applied only to structural and envelope assemblies within LEED, we anticipate that other types of assemblies and products, specifically building materials, may be pursued in future versions of LEED, so be sure to check the most recent version for your project.

After the pilot phase (in progress as of publication), it is expected that projects will be able to receive up to five points, depending on their LCA score for building assemblies. The intent of this credit is to identify and calculate environmental impact estimates for generic assemblies used in a project from the following assembly groups: columns and beams, floors, exterior walls, windows, interior walls, and roofs. These impact estimates will get entered into the USGBC Credit Calculator to produce the LCA impact score and the corresponding LEED points that could potentially be awarded. The assemblies will then be ranked according to their environmental impact and LEED credits awarded accordingly. This approach will provide a relatively quick yet significant infusion of LCA within LEED,

without having to wait for comprehensive standardization, thus enabling the LEED rating system to incorporate the first phase of LCA and encourage future adoption and standardization as the system matures further. USGBC's long-term objective is to make LCA a credible component of integrated design, ensuring that the environmental performance of the whole building takes into account the complete building life cycle.

To calculate LCA, the USGBC has adopted the Athena Institute's EcoCalculator for Assemblies.[43] This tool was developed by the Athena Institute in association with the University of Minnesota and Morrison Hershfield Consulting Engineers. The EcoCalculator has been well tested as the primary LCA tool for another building rating system—the Green Building Initiative (GBI) uses it for its Green Globes™ environmental assessment and rating system. The EcoCalculator creates instant access to LCA results for hundreds of common building assemblies. The results embedded in the tool are based on detailed assessments completed with the Athena Impact Estimator for buildings, which in turn uses Athena's datasets and data from the U.S. Life Cycle Inventory Database.[44]

Life Cycle Thinking

As consumers, we can (and should) begin to look for life cycle information regarding the products and services we buy: What kind of energy is used? What are the labor conditions? Does the manufacturing process generate hazardous waste? Are ecosystems endangered? Are air and water polluted during the process? We can be active consumers and try to find out if the businesses we regularly buy from have initiatives in place to address these types of issues and look for ways to support those efforts by purchasing their products.

Unfortunately, the problem with this approach is that it is nearly impossible to tell what a company's environmental practices and impacts are at the point of purchase, and you likely don't have time to do the research on each product you buy. Even so, these are issues to start thinking about as sustainability becomes more widely incorporated and intertwined with the daily products in our lives.

While formal life cycle tools are still being developed, we need to employ *life cycle thinking* into our professional lives in much the same way as the consumer approach just described. Below are some suggestions for incorporating life cycle thinking into your business in general, as well as what you can do with respect to product selection and project design to make more informed environmental decisions.

Life Cycle Thinking in Materials Selection

Life cycle thinking in materials selection requires more than simply knowing how to select the most environmentally friendly products. It also involves being an advocate for reliable, transparent information. Inquire if you think you need additional information to make an informed choice; request additional data as you feel is appropriate; and support and purchase products that not only make claims, but back the claims up with data and third-party certifications. You can:

- Specify and purchase products and services that are "environmentally preferable." This helps reduce the impact your products have on the environment and supports the development of regional and global markets for "preferable" products and services.
- Promote the accurate costing of products that you specify. Begin to truly assess the costs of environmental degradation, health problems, erosion of social welfare, and impacts at all life cycle stages of your product selection.
- Encourage manufacturers of products that can not currently be recycled to create a take-back system where they will accept return of the product at the end of its useful life to recycle or downcycle the product, whenever possible.
- Ask questions. Even these few will help you apply life cycle thinking the next time you are selecting products for a project:
  - What are the raw materials and where do they come from (rapidly renewable, recycled content, etc.)?

- How and where is the product manufactured (energy used, water used/recycled, waste created)?
- How does it get from there to here?
- How is it installed?
- How durable is the product and will it need to be replaced often?
- What are the maintenance procedures and chemicals/solutions used?
- What happens at the end of its life? Is it destined for a landfill? Can it be reused or recycled?

Manufacturers should be able to answer these basic questions. If they cannot, consider alternatives.

Life Cycle Thinking in Design

You can incorporate life cycle thinking into the entire design process by considering how to reduce, reuse, and recycle at every step in the design process. Recognize that each choice will have an affect at numerous levels. Your selections should address not only how the product will look and function, but also how the creation of that product will impact both the local and global environments as well as the particular community in which the product is manufactured, used, and either disposed of, reused or recycled. You can even inquire about a manufacturer's suppliers and their life cycle information.

For each aspect of design, try to :

- Rethink products and their functions in the project. Using the product more efficiently whenever possible will reduce the use of energy and other natural resources.
- Reduce energy and material consumption throughout a product's life cycle.
- Replace harmful substances with more environmentally friendly alternatives.
- Recycle. Select materials that can be recycled and build the product such that it is more easily disassembled for recycling.
- Reuse. Design the project and select products so that parts can be reused.
- Repair. Consider ease of repair in design so that products do not need to be replaced fully.

Life Cycle Thinking and Your Business

When you bring life cycle thinking into your business, tangible returns can be seen from marketing, branding, and reputation. Consider the following:

- Enhance your company and the value of your brands by implementing life cycle thinking. Businesses can avoid criticism and participate in issues beyond their direct sphere of influence by understanding the full spectrum of life cycle issues associated with their products, purchases, and processes. In fact, financial indices such as the Dow Jones Sustainability Indexes (DJSI) track and report the financial performance of leading sustainability-driven businesses worldwide.

- Find new ways for your marketing and sales departments to communicate and interact with customers. Some 50% of businesses—some of which are likely your clients—say they are interested in learning about sustainability.
- Share life cycle information with your suppliers, customers, and waste handlers to identify risks and opportunities for improvement.

Overall, life cycle thinking can promote a more sustainable rate of both production and consumption. Life cycle thinking can also help optimize the use of limited financial and natural resources. Designers and project teams can have an increased impact on a variety of levels not traditionally seen as their "scope." Through this widened lens, the customers that consume and communities that produce our specified products (near and far) are within our range of influence. We can encourage healthy and safe working conditions for product manufacturers and suppliers around the world. We can also create fewer overall negative environmental impacts in our construction processes. All of these benefits can be realized by optimizing design and product selection. In the process, we also derive more benefit from the time, money, and materials we use.

Making life cycle thinking an integral part of how we design projects, select products, deliver services, and decide what to consume (or what not to consume) will help to end—and possibly reverse—some of the current trends that are so damaging to our environment. Every decision counts.

Summary

Life cycle assessment and life cycle thinking can be boiled down to a few key principles for selecting the products and materials we use based on educated, reliable decisions.

- Define what matters most to you and/or your client from an environmental, economic, and aesthetic perspective.
- Look for certifications, but be astute in evaluating what they really mean.
- Access reliable, objective resources for information.
- Know what questions to ask.
- Recognize that there is no perfect material or product.
- Understand that there is no single industry database or tool that has been widely adopted for LCA.
- Choose products that meet performance requirements, fit the budget, and meet the aesthetic goals of the project.

- Remember that every decision counts.

Now that we have explored the various options in green building standards and rating systems, how they each recognize credits for building materials, and the certification bodies available to assess different materials, it is time to dive into specific material categories to see how these credits and assessments apply. The remaining chapters of this book examine, from the standpoint of "greenness" and "sustainability", the primary materials used in building composition.

We begin in Chapter 5 by reviewing foundational structural materials, then progress in subsequent chapters through primary interior building construction materials, finishes, paints and coatings, and furnishings. Each of these building materials has different requirements in terms of cost, aesthetics, durability, and sustainable features. While we may not be concerned with the look of foundational concrete or insulation, we're likely to be very concerned about its durability. Similarly, the cost of paint may not be as critical to us as the health impacts and effects on indoor air quality that paint can produce.

We will take a look at each building product and consider its specific benefits and drawbacks in terms of its sustainable characteristics. We will also review what new products have become available that offer healthier or more environmentally-friendly features.

Other Resources

In addition to the resources already noted in this chapter, we recommend the following:

The American Center for Life Cycle Assessment (ACLCA): *Formed in 2001, the mission of this nonprofit membership organization is to build capacity and knowledge of LCA. ACLCA is part of the Institute for Environmental Research and Education (IERE), a 501(c)3 organization. www.lca-center.org*

The Society of Environmental Toxicology and Chemistry (SETAC): *This not-for-profit professional society was established to promote the use of a multidisciplinary approach to solve problems pertaining to the impact of chemicals and technology on the environment. SETAC has taken a leading role in the development of Life Cycle Management (LCM) and the methodology of Life Cycle Assessment (LCA). setac.org*

Life Cycle Inventory Database by the National Renewable Energy Laboratory (LCI): *The LCI Database is publicly available and contains data modules for commonly used materials and processes. www.nrel.gov/lci*

Chapter 5: Structural Materials

Concrete and steel have become the standard for foundation materials in commercial building construction. It is hard to envision a building project today that does not make use of these widely available construction mainstays. Millions of tons of each are used every year, and their widespread commercial availability and popularity have helped to keep them relatively inexpensive considering how critical they are to the structure itself. On the other hand, they are also extremely heavy and delivering them to the job site is transportation intense.

This combination of significant weight and minimal cost typically causes a material to rate low on the sustainability scale. Concrete and steel are no exceptions. Transporting heavy materials that cost very little can put a huge carbon (CO_2) tag on the materials, especially when compounded by the fact that the manufacturing processes of these specific materials are already carbon intense. Finding sustainable alternatives to these base structural materials is a fairly difficult task, particularly given that they are such an integral part of build-

ings. Alternative materials are being developed, but it will take time before their quality can be tested sufficiently within a variety of assemblies to demonstrate their viability—and widespread adoption of these new, alternative materials depends, of course, on the success of these tests.

In the meantime, in the absence of proven alternatives, sustainability must be addressed in another way: by strategically making decisions about the materials that are selected.

Composition of Concrete

Concrete, one of the most widely available and used man-made construction materials, is frequently specified for a variety of applications including roadways, building foundations, walls, and flooring structures. Concrete can be transported in its liquid form, as pre-cast blocks, or as Insulated Concrete Forms (ICFs).

Concrete is created from aggregates, or crushed stone, such as granite or gravel. These bits are solidified with a

> *Concrete is commonly confused with cement; however the two materials are not the same. Concrete is composed of several different materials. One of these is cement, the binding material that hardens the concrete.*

binding agent, typically Portland cement. Portland cement is a hydraulic cement made by heating a mixture of various minerals from quarried rock, limestone, and clay in a kiln at very high temperatures to form a material called clinker, then pulverizing the resulting material and mixing it with gypsum. As the material calcines and the moisture evaporates, some of the carbonates and compounds within the mixture break down. At the end of the process, only 2/3 of the original mixture remains. The production process for Portland cement—a process that is both energy-intensive and relatively inefficient—is responsible for roughly 5% of all human CO_2 emissions.

Portland cement generally comprises 10–15% of the concrete mix. The concrete mix reacts with water, via a process called hydration, hardening the material to achieve the desirable strength. Binders other than Portland cement can also be used as supplemental hardeners. These alternatives, such as fly ash and slag cement, help minimize the quantity of the Portland cement needed for a concrete mix. As noted above, Portland cement has a high level of embodied energy and its production causes a substantial amount of CO_2 emission. Consequently, minimizing the amount required to harden concrete is desirable.

In addition to the high level of embodied energy attributed to the Portland cement component of concrete, the mixture must also cure, which typically takes five to seven days under the appropriate environmental conditions. Because a contractor must wait up to a week after pouring the concrete to move on to the next phase of a construction project, time is a real consideration as well.

Composition of Steel

Steel is used in an array of construction applications, such as road and bridge reinforcement, building foundations, structural framing, beams, nails, and screws. The transportation industry also depends heavily on steel, a fact that becomes especially apparent when you consider the ships, trucks, automobiles, and railways both built from it and required to transport the steel to its application site.

An alloy, consisting mainly of iron and (typically) carbon, steel is formed by smelting iron ore at temperatures in excess of 1300 degrees Celsius. Iron can be alloyed with other materials as well, but the iron-carbon alloy carbon steel is the most popular, accounting for over 90% of the steel produced today.

Traditionally, steel was produced in blast furnaces or basic oxygen furnaces, where the raw material entered the top of the furnace while air was supplied to the bottom, allowing the necessary chemical reactions to occur within the furnace as the material journeyed through. After World War II, electric arc furnaces (which heat the ores by using an electric current) began to gain a foothold in the steelmaking industry, ultimately replacing the old technology in the last several decades of the twentieth century. Electric arc furnaces typically use scrap metal as their source of material rather than producing raw steel from iron ore. The electric arc furnace is much more efficient than either blast or basic oxygen furnaces, requiring approximately 1/4 of the energy that was necessary in the older steelmaking technologies.

Concerns and Objections

Despite their use as the primary building materials in commercial construction, fundamental concerns exist regarding the sustainability of both concrete and steel. From a sustainability perspective, one major concern associated with any heavy, widely used material is the embodied energy required to extract the material and transport it. Transportation costs may well end up being as much as the material costs and thus represent a significant portion of the total price tag for the product. For example, if drywall costs $.10/sq. ft. in material cost, the transportation to get it to the job site could cost another $.10/sq. ft., thereby doubling the total delivered product cost.

Both concrete and steel require a high temperature (and therefore high energy) heating process to form each base material. These processes result in low cost, high embodied energy products that are equated to good value, prompting the specification of these materials and their transport to thousands of job sites around the world. Transportation costs often dwarf the actual material costs. This is true of both the starting materials—for example, the iron ore being delivered to the steel mill—as well as the finished goods, such as the steel beams being transported to the job site.

It should also be reiterated that steel is fundamentally based on iron ore, a naturally occurring material found on the earth. This ore is a finite resource and cannot be used indefinitely. Therefore, building materials that use raw iron ore are, by definition, not sustainable.

Alternatives/Best Choices

Given the environmental concerns attending steel and concrete as basic construction materials, what strategic choices can be made to ensure that the most environmentally savvy selections are made for materials that will comprise the bulk of construction projects?

First, let's address the transportation issues. In order to minimize the expended energy used in transportation, it is best to choose a manufacturing and shipping site that is close to the job site. This will minimize the distance that any delivery truck, rail line, or other form of transportation must cover, reducing the CO_2 emissions associated with the material overall. It's important to evaluate this carefully, however, because the impact of transportation on sustainability calculations is a multi-layered subject. It does no good to choose a manufacturing source two miles away from your facility on the East Coast if your supplier sources its raw materials from California and that material was originally extracted in China. That process chain would clearly miss the intent of purchasing something regionally in order to minimize the transportation CO_2 impact. Understanding the whole sourcing line of any material is essential to making wise choices that support sustainability goals.

Next, let's examine the production issues. In order to minimize the use of raw materials, and therefore the energy needed for extraction, it is best to maximize the amount of recycled content in the material. Steel is the most widely recycled material. Construction grade steel made over 90% recycled content can be commonly found. In addition to eliminating the energy needed to extract the ore, the energy required to recycle steel is nearly a quarter of the energy required to produce steel for the first time.

Similarly, concrete mix is available with fly ash. This by-product of coal production can replace nearly 30% of the Portland cement in the concrete. Fly ash is also commonly used as a binding agent in other materials, such as gypsum wallboard. Note, however, that because fly ash is recaptured in coal plant stacks and diverted from disposal, some concerns are being voiced about whether it is a safe material and what role it plays in the coal industry. These concerns center around the possible leaching of chemicals into materials and, ultimately, into the user environment.

Trends and Evolution

While alternative materials may someday completely replace the need for Portland cement in concrete, the new options currently in development have not yet been proven commercially viable. Similarly, a promising movement to convert the majority of steel production to recycled steel as its primary material source is well underway.

Because these two materials form the structural basis for most buildings, it is obviously not safe for an untested or unproven material to make its way into the marketplace or into a specific project simply because it has more sustainable attributes. Safety is the most important factor in buildings, so when making decisions about infrastructure, it is essential that you choose structural materials that have been tested for safety to the fullest extent.

Any company that plans to come to market with a replacement for basic building blocks, such as concrete and steel, must have an integrated business plan that includes a budget for large-scale testing and adherence to structural standards and building codes. Only when this has been successfully achieved will we see these conventional materials phased out in favor of more sustainable alternatives. In the meantime, the most conscious choices that can be made favor local or regional materials that minimize the energy needed for transportation, and materials with high recycled content.

Chapter 6: Wall Systems—Framing, Insulation, Wallboard, and SIPs

Once the exterior shell of a structure is complete, the focus turns to the interior construction—the ceilings, walls, and partitions that divide the structure into separate areas. We don't think about walls and ceilings as much more than that: dividers of space. In reality, however, these elements house much of the infrastructure required for the building to operate. Most frequently, wall and ceiling construction is accomplished through structural framing, with wallboard screwed to the framing members. (Some types of buildings are constructed mainly from concrete block and poured concrete, which we've addressed in Chapter 5.)

Water pipes, electrical conduit, cabling, and HVAC run rampant through the walls and ceilings of most buildings. While these systems are, for the most part, unseen, the building's occupants are highly dependent on all of them functioning correctly. In addition to these primary systems, another critical element hidden within the walls is insulation, stuffed in between the sheets of drywall, typically made of fiberglass,

and used for thermal comfort and, in some cases, noise abatement. So often, walls appear as a smooth, blank canvas awaiting the family portrait or the corporate value statement. In reality, however, they are assemblies of various materials that can have a significant impact on a building's interior environment. This chapter explores the materials used to construct walls and ceilings as well as the materials most commonly concealed behind them.

Framing

Let's start by looking at a standard wall assembly. As a wall is framed out, a top plate and a bottom (or base) plate are laid horizontally on the floor and ceiling. These plates provide the infrastructure to which the structural studs are attached. Studs can be wood, either 2x4 or 2x6 (these are nominal dimensions, actually measured dimensions are smaller) or steel, either 3 1/2" or 5 1/2". Typically, studs are spaced either 16" apart or 24" on center for the length of the wall. Insulation is stuffed in the wall cavity between the studs. (More will be said about various types of insulation later in this chapter.)

Similarly, ceiling construction is typically framed out using wooden or metal joists spaced 16" or 24" apart and the cavity filled with a slightly denser (and possibly thicker) insulation in residential applications. Commercial construction can be done similarly, or concrete slabs could be used. The ceiling application depends on what type of format is used. Open ceilings or dropped ceilings are the most common and each will have different insulation methods.

Composition of Metal Studs and Wood Studs

Light gauge steel is the primary material in metal wall studs. As we noted, steel is one of the more easily recycled materials and, therefore, one of the most widely available materials found in recycled form. In fact, steel is the most widely recycled material in the world. Recycled content for steel framing and beams can range from 30%–95%, and the amount of steel that is recycled after its initial application is close to 100%. Virgin steel often costs nearly four times as much as its recycled counterpart. Therefore, the simplest and most cost-effective option when choosing any steel product is to select the one with the highest recycled content.

Typically, inexpensive softwoods such as Douglas fir, pine, or spruce are used in framing. The wood used in wood studs is found in the outer layer of the tree, just inside the bark. This part of the tree is strong enough for framing and more plentiful than the denser inner portion of the tree, which is stronger and will be used for planks, structural lumber, or beams.

Concerns and Objections

When it comes to framing materials, a great debate exists over whether wood or metal studs are more sustainable. Those favoring wood framing argue that wood (1) is naturally occurring; (2) has a very low embodied energy; (3) does not incur thermal bridging; and (4) is sturdier than metal studs. The disadvantages of wood framing are typically that (1) it is a finite resource and (2) it is not sustainably harvested in many cases.

In contrast, those favoring steel studs point to the fact that the material is (1) widely recycled; (2) not harvested from virgin resources; (3) does not warp under exposure to certain climates and conditions; and (4) is generally more cost effective. The disadvantages of steel framing are (1) it is a finite resource; (2) raw material extraction is energy intensive; and (3) the demand for steel is so great that it can have a significant impact on the economics of transportation and carbon costs in sourcing the material from various sites.

Pros and cons to both arguments exist, and deciding what type of stud to use can be based largely on the construction needs and preferences of the contractors or architects involved in the project. Sustainable choices for each type of stud are possible, regardless of whether you choose wood or steel studs for wall construction.

Alternatives/Best Choices

Wood framing is available as a sustainably harvested material. The Forest Stewardship Council (FSC) is the most recognized entity offering third-party certification that designates products as sustainably harvested according to strict environmental guidelines. FSC certification, widely adopted by the industry and referenced by many of the building guidelines discussed in this book (including both LEED and Green Globes), is available for most wood products. Other wood certification bodies are being incorporated into building standards, so it is wise to consult the latest guidelines to see which other certifications are being accepted. Also, refer to Chapter 3 to review all the wood based certifications available at the time this book went to press.

Steel framing can be procured with high quantities of recycled content, typically around 30%; structural beams can have even higher levels of recycled content. All steel beams and framing can be recycled at the end of their useful lives. The disposal of materials is not always incorporated as a consideration in material selection, however green building discussions have broadened the scope accordingly to include new criteria that account for material disposal, reuse, and recycling at the end of its useful life.

Both wood and steel framing structural members can often be found locally, although not in all cases. As delineated in the U.S. Green Building Council's LEED rating system regarding Materials and Resources: Regional Materials credits (see MRc5), it is best to identify as early as possible in the construction process a supplier that either harvests or manufactures the chosen products within a 500-mile radius of the construction site. Other building standards include their own criteria for local content; however, the LEED criteria impose requirements comparable to those of most of the other standards. Some sustainable building methodologies can be implemented as standard construction techniques when building with either type of framing material. These methodologies include eliminating headers where they are not needed in non-structural walls, as well as increasing stud spacing from 16 OC (on center) to 24 OC in accordance with applicable building codes and corresponding stud thickness. Both methodologies use less material. Additionally, using engineered lumber, wherever feasible, can reduce the amount of old growth trees consumed for structural lumber and provide another way to increase the sustainability factor of your projects.

Trends and Evolution

As sustainable harvesting practices become more widespread, FSC and other certification bodies will continue to emerge. And, as such standards become more widely adopted, they will promote increased availability and acceptance of lumber that meets these criteria. The degree of oversight afforded by the certification process, accompanied by increased levels of project responsibility for making sustainable choices, will reduce the environmental impacts caused by uncontrolled logging practices and the resulting deforestation.

The increase in construction rates internationally over the past few decades created a high demand for steel in the late 1990s and the early part of this century. This rise in market demand drew attention to the limited and possibly constrained availability of steel in the future. It is likely that this awareness will encourage further growth in the already active recycled steel segment of the steel industry. As steel reclamation processes continue to be refined, we can hope to have more energy-efficient and even higher recycled content steel materials available in the future. Additionally, some manufacturers have found ways to use a patterned press to create steel of greater dimensional stability using less material. These practices and innovations, coupled with more efficient manufacturing processes, should lead to increasingly streamlined materials in the near future.

Insulation

As we all learned in high school science, heat moves from a warmer area to a cooler area through convection, conduction, or radiation. In the winter, this means that the efforts (or energy or money) put into heating a home or other building are lost, in part, through the exterior envelope or the exterior walls. Likewise, in the summer, the efforts (or BTUs or dollars) to cool interior building spaces battle with the heat moving into the structure from the outside through the walls.

Air flow is largely responsible for this phenomenon. Inhibiting air flow helps minimize the amount of heat lost or gained through some form of transmission to the outside. Heating and cooling can be responsible for up to 70% of a home's energy needs, meaning that an inefficient building envelope basically encourages money to flow directly out of the structure. Insulation stuffed in the wall cavity, interior or exterior, interrupts the air flow and prevents heat or cooling loss to a space at another temperature.

Composition of Insulation

Historically, fiberglass has been the most common insulating material. The glass fibers are formed from silica sand, limestone, and soda ash, which are melted and formed into batts (or blankets as they are often called). A batt, rolled up and shipped or stored in bags, is generally consistent in length with the wall height (8' or 96" is common). The width is usually slightly larger than the wall stud spacing, so the batt can be friction fit in the space and run the height of the wall to the ceiling.

Although there is little argument about the function of the insulation, substantial concern exists over its material properties. Fiberglass, once listed as a suspected carcinogen, is no longer; however, substantial safety concerns remain. With any type of insulation, it is imperative that installers or do-it-yourselfers adhere to the manufacturer's recommendations and guidelines for protecting oneself during the installation process. Because many of the health concerns associated with fiberglass relate to its installation, the question is raised as to what other options are available to insulate interior and exterior walls in a way that provides a healthier interior environment.

One alternative to fiberglass is cellulose insulation, which consists of a combination of ground news print and boric acid. Cellulose insulation is typically sprayed through a hose into a wall cavity with the intent of "filling in" the air gaps within the wall. The major concerns with cellulose insulation have been moisture-related as well as its propensity to settle over time, leaving a gap toward the top of the wall cavity once the material has settled toward the bottom. Spray-in loose-fill insulation is most commonly used where there is an existing space that has not been previously insulated. Due to the ease of application, loose-fill insulation can be the most practical, cost-effective option for adding insulation to a previously uninsulated space.

Mineral wool insulation, also called rock wool or slag wool, is formed from mineral mining waste that is subjected to a spinning process. This creates small fibers that are woven together to form the batts. Rock wool is formed from such rocks as basalt or diabase, both of which are igneous rocks formed by volcanic activity. Slag wool is created from iron ore mining waste. Mineral wool can have high levels of post-industrial recycled content; however, it can also have high heavy metal content as a result of its mining waste. A very effective vapor barrier in the envelope along with strict installation techniques should be employed to ensure minimal exposure to any potential heavy metal content.

Concerns and Objections

The major objections to all three types of insulation—fiberglass, cellulose, and mineral wool—center on exposure to unhealthy content, e.g., fiberglass fibers, possible mold in cellulose, or the heavy metals in mineral wool. Both fiberglass and mineral wool are composed of man-made synthetic fibers that have been extensively studied. Study results differ greatly, yielding inconclusive findings regarding the risks of exposure and potential health effects from these materials used in interior applications. Conducting due diligence on any insulation is your best bet before making a decision.

With spray-in materials, such as loose fill cellulose, there's an inherent risk (as noted earlier) that the material will settle over time as it becomes compressed. Like couch or bed pillows, this foam-like material has little structural integrity, which can be a major concern in walls where the purpose of the insulation is to inhibit air flow.

Another major consideration with insulating products is that while the materials in and of themselves are all bulky and low cost, transportation can be a major factor in the delivered (i.e., total) cost of the product. Transportation costs can add as much as 40% or more to the delivered product cost. Trucking companies typically consider weight a major factor in determining shipping costs. Thus, transporting an extremely lightweight material may not be as economical as it seems, because cost is based on cubic feet of shipping space.

Alternatives/Best Choices

As green standards and green building practices have emerged, they have, inevitably, provided impetus for the development of new green materials to replace their traditional counterparts. In the case of insulation, alternatives have emerged in both the types of materials used and the techniques employed. Spray foam insulation has become a front runner in sealing up the exteriors of the building (by spraying the foam on the inside of the walls), while new interior batt materials such as cotton have taken a leap forward as a healthier, more application-friendly alternative to fiberglass for sealing up interior wall cavities.

While formaldehyde-free fiberglass options are available as an alternative to the traditional fiberglass insulation, more natural alternatives also exist. For interior walls, for example, recycled denim insulation is one of the alternatives gaining market acceptance. Scraps from the denim manufacturing process are spun together with a rayon binder to create blue cotton batts, instantly recognizable as recycled denim and made from 85% recycled content. The company that makes the recycled denim insulation has achieved LEED Gold certification for its primary manufacturing locations. In addition to being a healthier alternative to fiberglass due to the lack of synthetic and invasive fibers, the material performs better acoustically as it is denser and heavier than traditional fiberglass batts. While acoustical benefits are not widely recognized yet in building standards, they are a significant factor in occupant satisfaction and productivity. The recycled denim, or cotton batts, are soaked in borates, which are naturally occurring chemical compounds used in a variety of household materials. The borates act as a natural fire retardant and the resulting materials are Class A fire-rated. The borates result in the cotton batts being mold, moisture, and pest resistant. Cotton insulation is available in the same standard thicknesses and R-values as traditional insulation. Wool insulation, formed from sheep's wool, another natural alternative to fiberglass, is rapidly renewable and provides qualities similar to denim.

In terms of the most efficient application for energy savings, the major focus is on the building shell as this is where most of the internal heating or cooling will be compromised. Because of this, the insulation techniques used on the building skin are the most important and affect thermal gain or loss significantly more than insulation used in the interior partitions.

Spray foam insulation is one of the fastest growing trends in exterior insulation. Available both as a petroleum-based product (which expands nearly one hundred times upon application) and as a bio-based material (typically derived from soybeans), spray foam insulation comes in both closed cell and open cell options and expands into all air gaps within the space, tightly sealing the building envelope. Closed cell insulation does not allow for air flow between spaces. The cells are basically encapsulated "bubbles" that prevent airflow thus making the material suitable for use in spaces that require both an air and moisture barrier. In contrast, open cell insulation allows for air and moisture to move between insulated spaces.

In selecting an insulation technique and product, there is always a balance to be struck between getting the most energy-efficient space and having the healthiest interior space. Achieving this balance adds complexity to the decision making process. The energy savings to the owner are crucial, but so are both interior comfort and a healthy interior space. Oftentimes, using the spray foam insulation to seal the roof deck and the exterior walls may be used in conjunction with a healthy batt product on the interior walls for good thermal and acoustic comfort, creating a hybrid approach to insulating the structure.

In addition, as previously discussed, transporting insulation can be costly and potentially dwarf the material cost. A good practice here, as with all insulation products, is to locate a manufacturing source as close to the project site as possible to minimize carbon costs and emissions associated with transportation.

Wallboard

Wallboard is the most widely used construction material in interior spaces. Wallboard is a broad category including all sheet goods typically mounted on a wall assembly. Of these, drywall (also called gypsum board), formed from a combination of calcium sulfate ($CaSO_4$) and water (H_2O), is the most common. The gypsum is often mined from ancient sea beds, making it a finite resource that does not replenish itself quickly. Eighty percent of the gypsum mined in the world is used as an ingredient in products such as drywall, plaster, gypsum concrete (for floor underlayments) and Portland cement (used in concrete, as described in Chapter 5).

Drywall is 90% gypsum and 10% paper. The paper is found on both sides of the drywall as the exterior surface to make material finishing, like priming and painting, easier.

The construction industry has historically used tens of billions of square feet of gypsum wallboard every year. Gypsum drywall is multifaceted in its use as wallboard in construction projects. It provides sound control thanks to its mass and resiliency, has inherent fire resistance thanks to the flammability properties of gypsum, and is easy to install by simply nailing or screwing the sheets to structural studs. Like concrete and steel, the widespread adoption of wallboard has given the product an incumbent's stronghold in construction projects—one that is unlikely to be challenged any time soon.

Concerns and Objections

Similar to stone or metals, gypsum is harvested through mining, giving rise to many related concerns, chief among them the disruption of surrounding habitats and the impacts on the local ecosystems around the extraction site. Additional concerns have also been voiced about worker health and safety issues.

Alternative approaches to gypsum exist that can potentially mitigate some of the issues further downstream in the wallboard supply chain. There are also some emerging materials that could address some of the upstream concerns as well. We'll address these downstream and upstream considerations next.

The manufacturing process for drywall is very energy intensive. The gypsum must be heated, in a process called calcining, to remove the excess water, which is then rehydrated into a slurry substance that will form the middle of the board. The slurry is laid out between two pieces of paper and finally kiln dried into sheets. Drywall poses the same dilemma as base construction materials such as concrete and steel; while it is a relatively low cost material, it weighs a lot and therefore presents comparable transportation issues. The delivered cost per pound can be as low as ten to fifteen cents (the cost of drywall varies greatly based on demand and supply). The carbon footprint of a sheet of drywall, already high due to the energy-intensive manufacturing process, is further exacerbated by the amount of energy required to get the heavy material to a job site. The transportation also often requires the use of an elevator or boom truck to carry the drywall to the necessary location within the building. Lastly, the disposal of drywall, either during deconstruction or as scrap material not used during construction, creates a huge amount of waste, and further potential to affect the environment.

Alternatives/Best Choices

Wallboard is manufactured in numerous gypsum plants throughout North America. When specifying gypsum wallboard, the best choice (and the approach that supports the highest degree of sustainability) is to purchase the material from a location close to the project site, thereby minimizing the shipping cost and corresponding carbon impact.

Alternatives to traditional gypsum wallboard include synthetic gypsum or recycled gypsum. Other recycled materials and some new products are currently undergoing testing and evaluation for use in wallboard products. Synthetic gypsum wallboard is composed of recycled gypsum as well as fly ash. The fly ash recovered from the desulphurization of coal stacks, combined with the recycled gypsum, creates wallboard that can achieve a recycled content of over 90%. Fly ash is readily available, with tens of millions of tons generated every year, over 70% of which is disposed of in landfills. Recycled gypsum drywall is a desirable material to use in synthetic or recycled products. However, because gypsum board is so inexpensive, it is rarely worth the time and energy involved in the tedious recycling process—you must separate the paper from the gypsum board and then extract just the middle-layer material to recycle into new boards. While this may be the most environmentally-conscious way to create an alternative product, it may not yet make sense economically. All issues, environmental and economic, need to be considered throughout any process that entails modifying old products or introducing new ones.

When choosing any type of drywall, pay close attention to the manufacturer's data to ensure that they are providing reliable and credible information. Material that does not have proper documentation could be dangerous or hazardous as evidenced by recent issues that have arisen with some Chinese drywall sources, where health problems have resulted from sulfur emissions produced by the drywall. Earlier we mentioned the drywall cuts and pieces often discarded as waste during a project. Since drywall comes in various widths and heights, it benefits the owner and/or contractor to carefully consider how to maximize cutting the material to minimize scrap and, therefore, waste. For example, choosing a 9-foot sheet of drywall, versus a sheet that is ten- or twelve feet high, can have a significant savings in overall cost for a project with an 8 1/2 foot ceiling.

If drywall waste is an unavoidable part of the project, look for a way to divert the unused material from the traditional waste stream (or landfill). Scrap drywall can actually be used as an effective fertilizer, as it contains natural minerals, calcium, and sulfurs, which are beneficial to soil and essential plant nutrients. This is one example of an inventive and insightful way to continue the usefulness of the product without the energy-intensive recycling process. It is also a great example of how to look beyond the traditional sphere of applications and see where else an opportunity may exist for innovation.

Alternative materials currently in research and development could eventually replace gypsum in wallboard altogether. However, as with concrete and steel, wallboard is a base material that serves as a fire barrier. For that reason, new products require extensive testing and performance measurement before they can be introduced for mainstream use. It is important to note, though, that these alternative products are well underway and could have a significant impact on the sustainable product movement by proving that the seemingly irreplaceable products can, in fact, be replaced.

Trends and Evolution

EcoRock, manufactured by Serious Materials, is a non-gypsum drywall material that has entered the marketplace with strong sustainability claims. These claims include touting a production process that uses 80% less energy than regular drywall manufacturing. Second, it reduces production-related CO_2 emissions by 80% versus regular drywall. And third, it is reputed to consist of 80% recycled content. EcoRock does not use the energy-intensive mining techniques and the product is currently not kiln dried; two strategies that help to drastically reduce energy emissions associated with EcoRock's manufacture. The company's factories, which are strategically located where the source materials are to be procured, are also designed to operate in a manner that minimizes their environmental impact and CO_2 emissions. While this alternative product is still undergoing testing in the built environment, the fact that these possibilities are being pursued at all is a testament to what can be achieved with the right focus on the environment. It also illustrates the potential for new products to successfully challenge old ones that have long been considered unchangeable.

New Wall Systems and SIPS

Choosing a wall system goes beyond the longstanding debate about whether wood or steel studs are more environmentally sound. One common technique gaining popularity has been tilt-wall construction, which is primarily a poured-in-place concrete slab that is tilted up in one solid piece to form the wall of a building. Tilt-wall structures are typically one- to two-story structures which can result in both reduced labor and operating costs for the building. The tilt-wall method is easy and quick.

It is worth noting that tilt-wall construction is no longer simply relegated to solid concrete. Other tilt-up and panel-based techniques that use different, lighter types of materials are emerging in the marketplace. For example, a layer of extruded polystyrene has recently been added between concrete layers to improve energy efficiency in the building envelope. It also helps to reduce the weight of the wall itself.

Similar to the insulation sandwiched between two layers of concrete described above, structured insulated panels (SIPs) use two layers of oriented strand board (OSB), plywood, or other sheathing material with a layer of foam insulation between them to create a panel product that performs as both an interior and exterior sheathing material. While this is the typical layer configuration of SIPs, modifications are possible to the interior (middle layer) material based on the particular building needs. The manufacturing process for SIPs has matured and the OSB material is familiar to contractors working with the product. This makes SIP development and implementation an evolutionary change to the building structure.

These panel products are used predominantly in light commercial or residential projects, where OSB sheathing is traditionally used in wood-framed construction. While the structural panels are mostly used in lieu of structural framing on the exterior of the house, interior uses are becoming more frequent. Non-structural versions of the panels are also being used more regularly, as there are solid benefits to the system (e.g., reduced labor costs associated with preassembly of the panels and energy efficiency improvements to the spaces or building envelope due to the sandwiched foam insulating layer). New, similar panel products are emerging frequently, also touting ease of installation and energy savings. As with any construction product, it's important to ensure that the required and appropriate testing has been completed for structural integrity, fire resistance, and both installer and user health and safety.

Wall Systems Summary

In this chapter, we have considered several wall system products and technologies that are not likely to see a major overhaul in the next several years. In selecting materials for our construction projects, we can always give preference to products that mitigate environmental impacts by manufacturing locally, achieving high recycled content, and optimally sizing materials to minimize waste.

Because several building blocks of the construction process (concrete, steel, and wallboard) share the combination of high weight and low cost, it is best to choose a product and supplier with the shortest shipping distance possible. In doing this, remember to think about not only the distance from the product supplier to your project site, but also about where the source materials have come from; the end user is inevitably charged for all shipping costs incurred along the way.

Manufacturers of nearly all construction materials are striving to increase the amount of recycled content in their products. For materials such as steel, this yields more cost-effective products than extracting new raw materials. The percentage of recycled content can be huge, making the choice of materials with high recycled content not only cost-effective, but also the best choice from a sustainability standpoint. Whenever possible, try to source local materials that also have a high recycled content from manufacturers in close proximity to your project site. Oftentimes, a manufacturer will advertise high recycled content material, but the plant may be located in Oregon when your project is in North Carolina. At that point, you must weigh the benefits of local materials against high recycled content and determine which has more value for your specific project.

For insulation, the options are increasing every day. Major objections to fiberglass abound, leading to an increasing awareness of softer alternative products for wall assemblies. Cotton, wool, no-added formaldehyde and recycled content options are readily available. They can each be evaluated and compared based on project needs.

Keep a look out for revolutionary new materials in these staple product lines. Creative minds and deep pockets are backing new materials that are queued up to make a run at some of the longstanding incumbents. These new alternatives offer a more eco-savvy package in all aspects—from their extraction and composition to their manufacture and transport.

Chapter 7: Flooring

In building construction, flooring is one of the categories where builders, contractors, and property owners enjoy a wide and ever-changing array of options. A single home, for example, will typically have at least three or four different types of flooring. In bathrooms and kitchens, flooring tends to be more durable, with an easy-to-clean surface that will hold up to high traffic, moisture, and spills. Hardwood or tile may be used in entryways and hallways. Living areas and bedrooms are often carpeted. It is quite common for homes to have a combination of flooring types depending both on personal preference and the function of each space.

Further, each category of flooring offers its own extensive array of options in terms of specific material, color, texture, size, thickness, surface finish, and so forth. With all of these flooring options now being forced to run the sustainability gauntlet and judged by the savvy green consumer, what considerations and changes must be made, and what new materials—or old materials with a new look—can enter the market to increase green and sustainable options?

Hardwood Flooring
Composition
A broad category, wood flooring encompasses various types of wood material. Solid wood flooring and engineered wood flooring are the most popular options. The former consists of a solid piece of one type of wood; the latter is produced by laminating a slice of solid wood to the top of a piece, or pieces, of a cheaper, softer wood, like plywood. In application, the cross-section of wood flooring can be a single solid piece or a series of strips of wood laminated together. The width of the plank can be narrow or wide, depending on the specification and construction needs, as can its thickness and length.

Regardless of the configuration of the flooring, a few issues will hold true for wood-based flooring types. Wood is a finite resource and hardwood trees have a long life cycle, typically requiring sixty to one hundred years to reach a size at which they can be harvested. For this reason, we must control the amount of wood we are harvesting to avoid depleting forests of already mature trees. The most popular species of wood flooring are oak, ash, and maple, followed closely by cherry and walnut. Many of the hardwoods sought for flooring are exotic species obtained from South America, Latin America, or Asia, such as Brazilian cherry, teak, and mahogany.

The other primary consideration in choosing wood flooring is whether it is pre-finished, unfinished, or, the more recently available, acrylic-impregnated. Acrylic-impregnated wood uses a finishing technique that forms a durable wear layer on the surface of the wood, enhancing its ability to hold up in high traffic areas such as hallways and entryways.

Concerns and Objections

Because hardwood trees can take over one hundred years to reach a harvestable size, it is an obviously limited resource. The booming popularity of hardwood flooring in recent decades has put a major strain on the amount of available resources relative to the demand.

In addition to the basic increase in demand, access to trees is limited if they are in a remote part of a forest. This often results in clear-cutting transportation paths to gain access to a coveted species. While some countries are active in preserving their forests, many are not. Mismanagement of forests lead to a loss of habitat for various animal species and, in many cases, a loss of habitat and livelihood for humans that inhabited and cultivated land sacrificed for logging purposes. Lack of consid-

eration for the forests by some entities in the lumber industry has resulted in several initiatives by locals to protect the forests, in addition to more widespread public involvement in many areas. However, these methods are by no means international requirements that dictate how forests are managed. In Chapter 3, we discussed some organizations that have been promulgating standards in an attempt encourage more sustainable harvesting and forest management practices. When it comes to forestry management, not only is the way that the trees are cut down an important consideration, but the overall practices in terms of labor, ecosystem, contamination, waste, and other environmental impacts. It is not enough to simply consider the number of trees that are logged and when, but rather, what is the overall impact of harvesting the materials. When trees are removed, soil erosion occurs; this can cause siltation of rivers and streams. Trees create oxygen and absorb carbon dioxide, a function integral and critical to healthy, balanced ecosystems. Following this logic, the continued consumption of the earth's forests inherently reduces the amount of CO_2 that can be absorbed and converted to oxygen.

Other concerns emerge further down the process chain of hardwood flooring. Regardless of whether the material is transported as logs or as precut lumber, transportation costs (particularly when lumber is shipped from overseas) as well as the carbon emitted during transportation can be high. Once transported, wood flooring can be further processed or pass through many different vendors before it actually arrives on a job site, resulting in more carbon emissions and transportation costs.

After arriving on a job site, the wood must be installed. The installation process is also a critical contributor to the sustainability considerations of the material, as the adhesives or glues used in installation could contain VOCs or the particular finish used could off-gas in the living space.

The intention here is not to invoke fear in thinking about using wood floors; it is important, however, that you note the concerns so that you can make educated choices and select the best options. Wood is a natural material, a great building resource, and when grown and harvested in an ecologically responsible manner, should continue to be an invaluable building resource for centuries to come. Several choices can be made when choosing wood flooring that will greatly increase the sustainability profile of the material, but only when that process entails sourcing the material from ecologically responsible providers and following the proper installation procedures.[45]

Alternatives/Best Choices

Below we lay out some wood-based alternatives to hardwood flooring made from newly harvested material. Following that discussion, we will explore non-wood flooring options such as bamboo, cork, rubber, linoleum, and carpet.

Reclaimed Wood

Throughout the U.S. and around the world, centuries-old structures exist that were constructed from some of the oldest and most durable trees in the forests at the time. Before steel took hold during the Industrial Revolution, solid wood beams served as the primary structural components of massive buildings and warehouses. Many of these buildings have served their purpose, cannot be reused and, as a result, the buildings are being torn down. Due to the age of these buildings, some may contain materials that are no longer permitted in working or living spaces—lead paint and asbestos, for example—further prompting owners to choose deconstruction over resale or reuse.

Deconstruction, by the nature of the word, is a much more environmentally conscious process than the more traditional *demolition* process. Deconstruction means the building is taken down carefully, rather than simply demolished, and its materials are either appropriately recycled or salvaged (e.g., brick, steel, and hardwoods) or disposed of properly (e.g., waste and hazardous materials). As deconstruction of buildings has become increasingly popular, the practice has created a great source of reclaimed hardwood flooring and beams that have been salvaged and are being sold for reuse. Many companies are emerging and maturing in the deconstruction and reclamation industries, giving customers a viable alternative for a sustainable material.

Previously used beams can be several feet thick and tens of feet long. The flooring in many old mills, distilleries, and warehouses is often solid wood. Subfloors of older buildings can be a solid three- or four-inch thick layer of hardwood, overlaid with a thinner hardwood floor.

Oak, maple, birch, beech, yellow longleaf pine, cherry, and black walnut, among others are the most common types of salvaged wood. The reclaimed material is quite often considered "recycled content," as it has served its original purpose and has not been recycled for use in a different or similar application. In some cases, previously used beams are re-sawn into flooring specified by a contractor or architect for a project; the reclaimed flooring will be carefully de-nailed, sanded, and refinished to meet project requirements. Uses for reclaimed wood are limitless and it puts no strain on existing forests. An additional upside to the use of reclaimed wood is its age. These materials typically came from old growth forests that were densely populated, resulting in tight growth rings in the trees and, therefore, dense, hard wood. A similar species grown today would not have the same density in its growth rings and thus would not provide the same hardness as reclaimed material in the same species.

Aesthetically, reclaimed wood has a certain character from the knots, growth rings, nail holes, and other features of old growth hardwoods that often occur naturally. The amount of character can be chosen based on the project's needs; some consumers want a clean smooth look, while others prefer the nicks and knots, feeling that they add character to the new space.

While reclaimed material is an easy option and the costs have come down significantly, sometimes this option is not economically viable, or volume constraints or other issues necessitate pursuing another option.

Sustainably Harvested Wood

How trees are harvested and the environmental impact of that process is the biggest sustainability issue when using wood-based materials. Harvesting wood in a way that is, at a minimum, neutral to (and ideally supplemental to) the supply of wood and trees would provide a solution to these particular sustainability issues. Several standards bodies have developed guidelines and requirements for employing sustainable harvesting. Best known, but by no means the only, are the Forest Stewardship Council (FSC) and the Sustainable Forestry Initiative (SFI). These groups have launched certification initiatives that address various factors involved in the harvesting of woods.

The certification systems have different requirements and considerations, making it difficult to do an apples-to-apples comparison to identify the most effective method. Currently, the FSC certification is the only one recognized by USGBC's LEED system; but, efforts are underway to make allowances for the inclusion of other certification systems based on the number of best practices and requirements each employs. An ideal certification system looks at how the material is planted and harvested (as well as when); plots the land and outlines harvesting requirements such that the net amount of wood in the area increases over time; considers the habitat, ecosystem, and other environmental impacts; and includes an auditing process to enforce compliance.

The premium on using certified wood has decreased dramatically over the past years, and most any type of wood is now available in a sustainably harvested form. Beyond flooring and lumber, most plywood, fiberboard, and chipboards are also available in a sustainably harvested form. Careful attention should be paid to standards bodies, like FSC and SFI, that have analyzed the various certification systems and adopted and encouraged the use of the ones they find the most rigorous and environmentally beneficial.

Engineered Flooring

Engineered flooring consists of a base material to which a veneer has been laminated. With engineered flooring, it is important to look at both the source of the wood material on top (the veneer) and also the base material to which it is laminated. The base material can be sustainably harvested soft wood, with a reclaimed or sustainably harvested hardwood layer on top. Consider the supply chain of all elements of the engineered floor, because some manufacturers use hardwood sourced locally but have a backing material that is applied overseas with formaldehyde-based glues. Be sure you ask the right questions about how engineered flooring is manufactured as you look at the various options available.

Laminate Flooring

Similar to engineered flooring, laminate flooring uses a thin top layer over a fiberboard backer to create a wood-like look. When choosing laminate flooring, it is best to consider the factors mentioned above, including its recycled content and sustainably harvested materials. Laminate flooring comes in a variety colors, and patterns and can emulate virtually any species of wood or other finish that a customer is looking for. Consider the base materials and make the greenest, the most sustainable choices, for the materials you use, including the adhesives that secure the layers to one another. Laminate flooring can be very smooth and easy to clean, which can make it attractive for minimizing allergens in a space.

Trends and Evolution

Reclaimed materials, such as salvaged wood, are being increasingly adopted for use in both new construction and renovations—this is the biggest trend. These reclaimed materials are popular thanks to their unique character, which cannot be replicated in new wood flooring from fresh cut lumber. While very little has changed in solid wood flooring selection, there have been significant advancements in the realm of engineered flooring and some of the materials used in its composition. Engineered flooring opportunities continue to evolve through a number of facets: new techniques are being developed to attach the hardwood layer to the engineered wood underneath; different layering techniques are being used to vary appearance and durability; and new adhesives are being adopted, ideally to minimize environmental impacts. For cost-conscious consumers, the use of engineered flooring creates the look of hardwood flooring at a lower price. This frugality has driven much of the innovation in engineered wood floors.

Non-Wood Alternatives to Wood Flooring

Having just outlined some positive choices that can be made to mitigate the impact of wood flooring on the environment by opting for local, recycled, or reclaimed materials, we turn your attention now to non-wood alternatives, which can also provide more sustainable flooring options. Many building standards recognize the use of materials that are considered rapidly renewable or have a growth cycle of less than ten years. (See Chapter 2 for a review of the different material credits available in various guidelines such as LEED, Green Globes, and NAHB's Green Building Standard, as well as how each standard treats material considerations.) While most hardwood trees can take over one hundred years to reach a harvestable size, rapidly renewable materials can be ready for harvest in a fraction of the time, resulting in a more readily available building product—one with less impact on the environment when it is cut down because it replenishes more quickly.

Bamboo
Composition

A grass that grows primarily in tropical regions, bamboo is a rapidly renewable material frequently used in construction applications. Because of its extremely high tensile strength, bamboo has been used in construction for thousands of years. In its native Asia, bamboo is used for scaffolding in lieu of the metal scaffolding typical in other countries.

The most common variety for construction purposes is Moso bamboo (Phyllostachys pubescens). Test groves have been planted in similar climates in non-Asian countries, including the U.S., but production volume does not yet come near the scale achievable in bamboo's indigenous regions.

Bamboo can grow up to eighty feet tall and three to seven inches in diameter. Moso bamboo can be harvested in five to six years (up to twenty times earlier than traditional hardwood forests, and also more frequently). Important, also, from an environmental standpoint, bamboo forests are critical to the balanced exchange of oxygen and carbon dioxide in the environment and can generate up to 35% more oxygen than the equivalent shade of trees.[46]

Concerns and Objections

While many bamboo flooring manufacturers have entered the market, the quality of product varies considerably. Look carefully for a well-established, proven provider of bamboo flooring, one that has tested its materials rigorously and published the results (there is no industry-approved designation, so it's just a matter of doing your homework). The best bamboo flooring and sheet good manufacturers adhere to the most advanced standards and proactively test their materials in advance of customer demands.

The harvesting practices of the bamboo supplier are also important to consider. Some suppliers engage in clear-cutting, thus damaging the environment; others use undesirable labor practices. If the practices are not transparent, or are unknown, it is best to find a supplier that can back up the claim that they use sustainable harvesting practices. Bamboo material is available that adheres to third-party–certified wood standards, such as FSC. Manufacturers should be able to provide certification specific to their bamboo products, not just a generic number that could pertain to other wood products they may offer.

As is true of all materials, trade-offs exist between the greener features of bamboo and its less sustainable characteristics. Its carbon footprint, for instance, is an important consideration. Most construction-grade bamboo used in flooring and millwork comes from China, where the material is indigenous. Transportation from China or other sources in Asia to the project site must be taken into consideration and weighed against the material's benefits: rapid renewability, possible FSC certification, and the availability of bamboo products with no added formaldehyde.

Alternatives/Best Choices

With a hardness rating up to twice that of some standard wood flooring, bamboo is a highly practical, not to mention attractive, flooring material. The larger plant stalks are milled into strips, which are then laminated together, either in a single layer or multiple layers to form flooring. Bamboo flooring is also available as a woven product, or a stranded version formed by pieces of bamboo mixed with a binder. This combination forms a commercial-grade product that can have a hardness rating twice that of traditional bamboo flooring and can be as much as three to four times harder than some solid wood flooring options. Bamboo flooring is available in two conventional colors: the natural, yellowish bamboo that we often see, and a carbonized or caramelized amber color that is simply baked to bring out the darker shade. Some darker stained options are also available, which can look as dark as black walnut or stained oak.

Trends and Evolution

Bamboo products are available as FSC certified, as well as with no added urea formaldehyde (NAF or NAUF). These options are good indicators of which providers are thinking about the sustainability of the product as a long-term business versus who are looking to make a quick dollar capitalizing on a new market.

Because commercial-grade bamboo flooring mentioned above is relatively new to the market, many people are not yet aware of this economical solution, targeted at high-traffic areas due to its increased hardness rating. However, use of this material is likely to continue to grow as new sustainable alternatives to non-wood products become increasingly sought after.

Cork

Composition

Another rapidly renewable material, cork is an ideal option when what's desired is a soft, warm, resilient flooring material that comes in a variety of colors and patterns. In fact, cork has been used as a durable and resilient surfacing option for hundreds of years, most notably for flooring. Famous installations of cork flooring include the Toronto Stock Exchange, First Congressional Church of Chicago, and the Library of Congress; many of these installations date back to the late nineteenth century.

The cork oak tree is the source, indigenous to and harvested predominantly in countries along the coast of the Mediterranean Sea such as Portugal, Spain, Italy, and France. North African countries including Tunisia and Algeria are also sources of cork oak bark. Once the tree has reached twenty-five years of age, the cork material can be harvested and then, going forward, every eight to fourteen years without causing any damage to the tree, which will re-grow its bark. The trees continue to live and grow for up to 300 years.

The process for harvesting the cork bark is relatively simple. In the summer months of June, July, and August a hatchet is used to strip bark from the mature trees (those at least twenty-five years old). The bark is stripped carefully so as not to damage an inner bark layer underneath. The bark slabs are then boiled and their rough outer layer removed, leaving behind a soft, resilient material that we commonly recognize as cork.

Cork forests are very beneficial to the biosphere, second only to the Amazon forests in their absorption of carbon dioxide from the environment. A cork oak tree that has been harvested or stripped of its cork bark can actually absorb up to five times the carbon dioxide as a tree that has not had its cork bark harvested. Cork harvesting is not only essential to the local ecosystem, it promotes biodiversity within its forests, which are home to hundreds of plant and animal species, some endangered, that depend on the unique attributes of these forests to survive. Because cork forests are so critical to the environment, the greatest danger actually comes from *not* harvesting the bark. Whereas the greatest consideration for other materials is over-harvesting, this consideration is entirely the opposite. It is difficult to argue with a material that increases its environmental benefit when harvested.

Cork has several unique attributes that make it suitable and desirable for flooring. One is its closed cell structure, which contains a gaseous substance. The gas is what allows the compressed cork to bounce back, resuming its original shape over time, much like small, closed bubbles that contract and expand when pressure is applied to them. Because cork is naturally resilient and provides substantial sound absorption, it makes great acoustical flooring. Cork also contains suberin, a substance that gives it a waxy look and feel and intrinsically resists bacteria, mold, and mildew, and also prevents rotting. Suberin renders the cork impervious to gas and liquids which, along with the closed cell structure, make the material ideal for wine bottle stoppers, which must have a good seal in order for the wine to keep and mature properly. These same properties serve well when cork is used in flooring applications. In addition to resilience and good acoustical properties, the closed cell structure gives cork its "warm" feel, literally acting as insulation and blocking cold from permeating the material.

Concerns and Objections

The introduction of the synthetic wine cork has resulted in less cork harvesting, which, as noted earlier, could actually have a negative environmental impact. Given this, finding alternative uses for cork, such as for building materials, is desirable and sensible. Although cork has been around for years, the shift away from real cork material for bottling applications has made it more available and viable from a supply/demand—not just an environmental—perspective.

From a performance standpoint, several factors need to be considered. Cork can yellow over time and fade in sunlight. It may also swell when it gets wet, making the material inappropriate for kitchen or bathroom applications—wet mopping is definitely not recommended. New finishes are being introduced in the cork world that can prevent some of these problems from occurring over time. As with any material, though, it is important to know what the maintenance requirements will be for a specific space and careful consideration should be taken when considering the finishes used to seal the cork flooring, using less toxic and no-VOC options when possible.

Alternatives/Best Choices

Cork flooring is available in a variety of patterns and colors, and comes in both interlocking planks and tiles. It can be glued down or used as a floating floor. Cork flooring is used in both residential and commercial applications due to its durability, high wear, and good acoustic performance. The finish on cork flooring ranges from a non-toxic oil finish to a more rugged vinyl finish to protect the material. When possible, it is best to use the more sustainable, environmentally friendly non-toxic finishes.

Trends and Evolution

Cork flooring has come a long way in recent years. As we mentioned earlier, the variety of patterns and aesthetics has increased dramatically and the combination of its look, acoustic performance, and durability has made cork a desirable option for any number of projects. Though cork has been used as flooring for hundreds of years, the recent awareness and emphasis on its environmental attributes, coupled with its inherent acoustic and anti-microbial attributes, has resulted in an increased use in high traffic areas of buildings and homes. With heightened attention being paid to acoustic comfort and sound transmission, soft materials like cork that are also durable are seeing increased applications as attractive and viable solutions to contribute to noise abatement. As cork flooring manufacturers continue to introduce more interesting styles and finishes, it is reasonable to expect that the adoption of cork as a sustainable flooring option will continue to escalate.

Rubber
Composition

When sound absorption and vibration reduction are important, rubber flooring is a good option. Rubber flooring comes in three basic types: synthetic, natural, and recycled.

Synthetic rubber flooring is derived from raw materials used in petroleum production. As such, it is the least sustainable of the three alternatives, having the greatest environmental impact due to its production and energy impact. There are several processes for creating synthetic rubber; most involve refining crude oil into a material called naphtha, which is then combined with natural gas to create monomers, which are, in turn, then combined to create chains of polymers (via polymerization or polycondensation). Due to the number of available monomers and possible combinations, several types of synthetic rubber can be created, each having its own particular properties.

Virgin, or natural rubber, is sourced directly from the latex tree and is 100% rapidly renewable. Natural latex is tapped from the tree in a manner similar to tapping sap from a maple tree. Natural rubber plantations are found predominantly in Thailand, Indonesia, Malaysia, and Sri Lanka.[47] This material can be used to form rubber tiles and flooring.

Recycled rubber is the greenest of the three options and has the lowest environmental impact due to the ease of production, since the material has already been formed into rubber. It is also cost-effective in comparison to extracting and shipping the new natural materials.

Concerns and Objections

The major drawback to rubber flooring is the off-gassing that can occur. The amount and toxicity of off-gassing depends on the type of flooring chosen. While recycled rubber flooring is the best choice overall for low environmental impact, it can off-gas more than other rubber flooring options. For this reason, it probably should not be used in an enclosed space. Recycled rubber from tires has an obvious odor and is a major culprit behind noxious fumes. These emissions can impact indoor air quality, so any space incorporating recycled rubber flooring should be well ventilated.

Alternatives/Best Choices

Rubber flooring provides a nearly seamless installation, with interlocking tiles that can be placed without the use of adhesives. When an adhesive is needed, it is best to choose a low or no-VOC. (See Chapter 11 for more information about adhesives.)

Capitalizing on its excellent wear and durability, slip resistance and traction, and resistance to fading, rubber flooring may be an ideal solution for a space that would benefit from those performance characteristics. Lastly, but certainly not to be overlooked, rubber flooring is 100% recyclable at the end of its lifetime.

Trends and Evolution

A myriad of style and color options in rubber flooring currently exist, giving designers an extensive gallery to choose from. Because it can so easily be recycled, rubber flooring provides a valid and attractive option for sustainable spaces. Given this, its range of uses is likely to expand. New options in rubber flooring should emerge—specifically for indoor use—that use recycled rubber and address the existing off-gassing problems typically associated with recycled tires. The elimination of PVC and chlorine-based recycled rubber should help speed the adoption of rubber flooring in interior spaces. Schools and health care settings are ideal applications (once any off-gassing concerns are addressed), due to the combination of shock absorption and sound attenuation properties of the softer rubber flooring, which is also naturally and conveniently slip-resistant. Lastly, the durability of the material gives it a long life cycle, an attribute that contributes to the material's sustainability features.

Linoleum
Composition

A natural building product, linoleum is made from cork, wood dust, linseed oil (derived from the flax plant), pine rosin, crushed minerals and limestone for color, and a jute backing material. In contrast, vinyl flooring (a material that often competes with linoleum in similar applications) is derived from several petroleum byproducts and is almost completely synthetic. The other major difference between the two materials is their color and patterning. While the pattern and color on vinyl flooring is on the surface only—essentially "printed" onto the top layer of the product—linoleum, which is a longer lasting product, has color that is mixed through it, making scratches and dings difficult to notice. Linoleum is available in either sheets or tiles and can be floated or glued down.

Concerns and Objections

One of the most environmentally unfriendly changes to flooring occurred in the 1950s when vinyl flooring largely displaced the use of linoleum in the flooring market. The products are similar in terms of their durability, life span, ease of maintenance and cleaning, and overall look and feel. Both are also soft underfoot and perform well in acoustically sensitive areas.

However, the environmental considerations for the two materials are substantially different. The natural composition of linoleum allows it to be recycled at the end of its lifetime. Vinyl flooring, on the other hand, cannot be easily recycled due to the complex combinations of synthetic materials that would need to be separated and broken down in order to be reused.

One drawback of linoleum is a temporary smell that's present after the material is installed. The odor comes from the natural materials used to create the sheets or tiles, namely the linseed oil. While not harmful, the odor can be unpleasant and inconvenient. Linoleum can also yellow temporarily—a phenomenon referred to as the "bloom effect." However, the color eventually returns, typically in a matter of days or weeks.

Alternatives/Best Choices

Linoleum flooring can be difficult to install because it needs to lay flat, flush against the wall, and be fastened accordingly. For best results, the material should be installed over a solid subfloor by a professional installer. Sealing and resealing the material, typically at least once per year, is also important to ensure easy maintenance and sustained quality. As with all flooring options, you'll want to carefully consider adhesive options. No-VOC or low-VOC adhesives are easy to use in the installation of linoleum products.

Trends and Evolution

With the renewed interest in environmentally conscious building materials, linoleum, with its natural base ingredients, has re-emerged as a viable and attractive flooring choice for sustainable structures. Many new looks and textures are now available, giving it a less dated look. Indeed, architects are able to create a modern look by incorporating linoleum into green projects, while still meeting the performance and design requirements of the space. Click-lock, or "floating" version of linoleum tile, is also increasingly available. This type of installation allows the floor to remain unattached to the subfloor below, mitigating noise and providing for ease of installation.

Carpet
Composition

Natural fiber choices for carpet material include not only animal-based fibers such as wool, but also several plant-based options such as sisal, sea grass, corn, coir, and jute. While alpaca and cashmere are animal fibers used to make carpets, by far the most popular of the animal-based fibers for carpeting is wool, which is 100% rapidly renewable and biodegradable. Wool is also naturally fire resistant, stain resistant, and anti-static. As a result, wool carpet, available either in rolls or in tiles, requires less chemical treatment during installation.

While not as common as their animal-fiber counterparts, several plant fibers are often used as carpeting materials. The most popular of these is sisal, which comes from the leaves of agave, a plant that grows in Latin America and the deserts of Africa. Sea grass, another plant fiber used in carpeting, must be used in its natural color, as it grows underwater and will not hold dye. Corn can be used in carpet manufacture after it is converted to starch, then into sugar, then into plastic, from which fibers are drawn and spun into a yarn. Coir, a material formed from coconut husks, is also used in carpet fibers, as is jute, a tree whose fibers are also commonly used in carpet-backing material. Depending on the intended application, drawbacks to plant-based carpeting options include the fact that they are not plush and many have moisture-retaining issues.

If bio-based fibers cannot be used, the next best option is to consider a carpet that is high in recycled content. Many progressive carpet manufacturers have launched programs to recycle old carpet and use the reclaimed material in new carpet or in carpet backing. In addition to recycling the carpet material itself, other recycled materials may be used and incorporated into the material. Plastic PET (polyethylene terephthalate) bottles, such as water and soda bottles, as well as textile fibers such as wool, cotton, hemp, and nylon, are also recycled and used in carpet manufacture.

Concerns and Objections

Over 70% of all floor space in the U.S. is covered with carpeting. Conventional carpet is one of the bad boys of the flooring industry. Unfortunately, carpet can be a significant contributor to unhealthy interior spaces due to its composition, the physical properties it holds in its final form, and the adhesives used to secure it in place.

The base material in conventional carpeting is a combination of petroleum-based synthetic materials, including acrylic, nylon, polyester, polypropylene, and synthetic styrene-butadiene latex. These materials consume a large amount of energy and result in significant pollution during their manufacturing process, typical of the petroleum industry. Many carpet products are backed with PVC, a material that is increasingly banned in a number of consumer products. SB latex, used in the majority of conventional carpet backing, contains styrene—or vinyl benzene—another suspected carcinogen, as labeled by the EPA.

Carpet is also heavily treated with chemicals to make it "consumer ready." These include fire retardants, fungicides, dyes, and anti-static as well as stain-resistant treatments, of which can all off-gas, as they contain VOCs and other harmful substances. Once installed, maintaining a carpet's appearance requires frequent cleaning or shampooing and vacuuming to prevent dust and allergens from building up, as well as to avoid mold and mildew from forming in the piles and on the strands.

Selecting carpet can be a complicated process. You have to consider its density, height of the pile, number of twists, stitching, weight, and durability. You also have to decide between rolled carpet and carpet tiles. Add to that the intention to select a carpet with green attributes and you introduce another multi-faceted dimension to the already complex decision-making process.

Alternatives/Best Choices

Despite all these concerns, viable and even desirable options for green carpeting exist. The most readily available is carpeting made from natural animal or plant fiber products, like wood, sisal, or seagrass. Another excellent option, noted previously, is carpeting that incorporates recycled materials.

When it comes to installation, better choices entail using no-VOC adhesives or tacking the material down instead of gluing it. Laying down carpet tile rather than rolled carpet allows for easier remediation and/or replacement of any damaged areas that may occur. For example, instead of having to replace an entire room of carpeting if something is spilled and creates a stubborn stain, you can simply remove a few tiles and replace them individually.

Fortunately, carpet has been at the forefront of standards efforts for environmental sustainability. The Carpet and Rug Institute's (CRI) Green Label program sets requirements for carpet pads; its Green Label Plus program sets the requirements for the carpets themselves. Additionally the National Sanitation Foundation (NSF) and the American National Standards Institute (ANSI) collaborated to develop the NSF/ANSI Standard 140-2007, which was designed as a certification system for green and sustainable carpet. The standard outlines performance requirements for healthy, environmentally friendly carpets and considers the "triple bottom line," looking at not only the environmental aspects, but the socio-economic benefits as well.

Trends and Evolution

Carpet has received a lot of attention thanks to its widespread popularity and the sustainable alternatives that are possible. Manufacturers have stepped up to provide viable and desirable options to consumers who want a healthy interior environment without foregoing the benefits of carpet to which they have become accustomed, while also looking internally at the environmental qualities of their manufacturing processes. A substantial number of changes are being made across the board in the manufacturing process and, by tackling issues of recycled content, installation, off-gassing, and end-of-life disposal, the carpet industry is also increasing environmentally-friendly options—those that improve the sustainability profile of the overall carpet market while providing consumers with the warmth and appeal they desire.

Tile, Stone, & Ceramics
Composition

Made from naturally occurring materials, stone and tile provide very durable flooring options. Available in an extensive color palette, tile and natural stone boast various patterns and figures and lend a relatively cool feel to spaces, particularly compared to other flooring options such as carpet and cork.

Stone varieties popular in flooring include slate, marble, limestone, travertine, flagstone, and granite. A great option in an area that can make use of its inherent qualities, stone (because it does not hold heat well) generally remains cooler than other flooring materials; it is naturally mold- and bacteria-resistant; and it is easy to clean and essentially scratchproof. Stone can be sandblasted, honed, polished, split-faced, brushed or otherwise finished, giving it a wide array of character possibilities.

Stone composites made from aggregates are another favorite for flooring applications. Engineered stone materials, or terrazzo, incorporate stone chips or other aggregates in a polymeric, concrete, or resin binder to be formed into tiles. Based on the pigments and aggregate sizes used, these tiles can be created in a nearly endless mix of colors and styles offering far more variety than naturally occurring stone. Yet, because the base material is aggregate (typically from stone), terrazzo often provides much the same durability as its solid stone counterparts.

Engineered stone materials can be formed into tile or poured. It is up to the owner, architect, or contractor which type of material is used as each has its particular benefits. Terrazzo tiles also often use colored glass in the mixture, the best choice being recycled glass. Post-consumer glass from wine, beer, and soda bottles is often readily available. Glass from post-industrial processes, pre-consumer glass from windshields or glassware, and ceramic and porcelain chips from dish-making processes are all used to create an array of looks in engineered flooring options.

Clay and other earth-based materials are also used to make ceramic or porcelain tiles for additional flooring options. Ceramic tiles can be either glazed (the most common option) or unglazed in their final form. Glazing tiles introduces minerals and dyes in the form of a top layer of glass, giving the tile additional color and texture. The tile is then fired (often multiple times) to achieve hardness and to create either a gloss, semi-gloss, or matte finish. Most often ceramic tiles are smooth-textured, making them easy to clean. Their surface is impermeable and nonporous after the firing process.

Porcelain tile undergoes the same process, but because it is made from 50% feldspar and more refined clay materials it requires a higher firing temperature, resulting in a much harder material than ceramic. Porcelain is also denser because the starting materials are more refined, pure, and uniform, and thus make the finished product less susceptible to water absorption. Like ceramic, porcelain is available glazed; however, a relatively new process that results in a solid color throughout the tile is becoming increasingly popular. This newer process allows the porcelain tile to stand up to heavier wear than ceramic tile as any scratching or chipping on the surface reveals the same color below.

Poured concrete and concrete tiles are also favorable options for flooring material. With poured installation, keep in mind that a cure time is necessary to allow the material to set which could potentially impact construction schedules. When using poured materials, the greener choices are similar to those discussed in the concrete section (see Chapter 5), where using local materials to minimize transportation costs is best. Opting for the material with the highest recycled content, such as fly ash and recycled aggregate, is also is kinder to the environment.

Concerns and Objections

The durability and long lifetime of stone and tile products are persuasive arguments for their use. Provided that no major renovations occur in the space where they are placed, replacement won't be necessary for many years. The desirable properties of stone products must be balanced against concerns about how they are sourced: the extraction, production, and manufacturing methods that are employed as well as the transportation methods and distances.

While tile and stone are available in many areas worldwide, they are typically sourced from Europe and Asia, where they are mined, milled, or manufactured. Natural stone and some of the strip mining practices in various countries have come under fire for poor labor and environmental conditions, for blasting and extraction practices that can contaminate the surrounding ecosystem, and for runoff from the mines that creeps into local water sources. Mining practices of the stone must be considered in order to make the most environmentally conscious choice.

The weight of stone and tile is another factor that needs to be considered. Since stone and tile are incredibly heavy, they require a significant amount of embodied energy to transport to a job site. When transportation energy is coupled with the energy used in the extraction and manufacturing of the materials, the overall embodied energy and carbon impact of these heavy materials can be quite significant. The best choice to make when selecting stone is to opt for a mine or a source that is 500 miles or less from the project site. (The 500-mile radius is a sustainability standard set in the LEED materials guidelines. For more information, refer back to Chapter 1.) One possible issue with this radius standard is whether the look of locally sourced tile or stone provides the aesthetic desired for a particular project.

Alternatives/Best Choices

When selecting stone and/or tile, significant choices need to be made and many factors can affect how green or sustainable your choice truly is. The selected material should be durable, have a long life span, and the intention should be that the material will be used for a long time, thus capitalizing on that natural advantage. As we note, the transportation and energy costs of such a heavy material should be considered. In addition, engineered versions that use recycled material rather than requiring the mining of new materials is preferred, when available.

Trends and Evolution

Stone and tile have been used in construction for millennia primarily because of their durability and abundance and will continue to be popular in the trades for the foreseeable future. Ideally, we will see an increased use of reclaimed stone and recycled materials incorporated with crushed stone and other aggregates, making mining or quarrying less crucial. Tile manufacturers are continuing to incorporate an increasing amount of recycled content into their products and launching programs whereby tiles can be recycled at the end of their useful life by including them in other products or building materials, such as terrazzo or concrete countertops. The durability and long life of stone and tile are both key attributes driving their adoption in new green construction as long life cycle materials.

Summary

Choosing green flooring for a commercial or residential space is a significantly layered and multi-faceted process. It requires selecting from multiple product options based on the amount of foot traffic, size of the area, use of the space, moisture criteria, and other environmental conditions, not to mention the aesthetics desired. Overlaid on these requirements are the cost considerations for the materials and the installation, as well as the longer term implications of the floor's wear, durability, life cycle, and replacement costs.

Given the myriad issues to keep in mind, there is no "one size fits all" when you're tasked with choosing the ideal flooring material. However, demand for green alternatives is on the rise, leading to more and more materials for you to choose from, from eco-friendly versions of naturally-occurring materials, to man-made versions, such as engineered wood and vinyl. With even more sustainable flooring options to come, no doubt, it's easier than ever to choose "green" flooring.

Chapter 8: Countertops

Countertops occupy very little actual surface area in a residential or commercial space, most commonly in kitchens or bathrooms. However, they tend to play a large role in defining these spaces both physically and aesthetically. Countertops may also set the tone for the decor, and for that reason, can have a significant impact on the rest of the home or office spaces. For all of these reasons, it's not a bad idea to spend some time and thought selecting a countertop material.

The choice is not always an easy one. Not only do countertops need to be aesthetically appropriate to the space, they also have to perform well, be easy to maintain, and have exceptional durability—all at a cost that fits the budget. Most people are looking for a neat, clean palette on which to prepare, cook, and set up for meals, as well as a place to gather around for entertaining or socializing. These activities makes counter space, no matter the surface area, a critical one to the owner, as it can often be a focal point of the room and a hub for the entire home.

The evolution of countertops has been an interesting one. Laminate or Formica countertops have been the de facto standard for much of the last century in both residential and commercial applications.

Over time, however, preferences and styles have changed. The common progression has been from Formica to granite, which has become frequent in many mid- to high-end homes. Other options include solid surface materials, which, for our purposes, will be considered as those that are predominantly made from high-tech plastics such as Corian, Dural, and Avonite. While engineered stone has emerged as an alternative, natural stone continues to have a strong presence in higher end homes, along with concrete composites and a new suite of green options. As always, laminate manufacturers, taking advantage of the material's capacity for diverse patterning options, are adapting their product to mimic what's most popular.

In this chapter, we'll review issues associated with a variety of countertop materials including laminates, solid surfaces, engineered stone, natural stone, concrete, and stainless steel.

Laminates

Laminate countertops are frequently the most cost-effective option. They are also easy to clean and come in an extensive palette of colors and textures that can emulate granite, marble, concrete, and many other natural materials. Despite their chameleon-like appearance, laminate sheets have a standard composition, typically formed in three layers. The bottom layer is Kraft paper, which is the heavy, brown paper material used in grocery bags, combined with some packing paper soaked in phenolic resin. The middle layer contains the various color and pattern options depending on the specific selection of the laminate. The top layer is a clear coat for durability and finish. The three layers are fused together using heat and pressure to form the final laminate sheets. Once cut to size, the sheet is then adhered to a backing material—typically medium-density fiberboard (MDF)—to form the countertop. It is basically a sheet of plastic adhered to a wood-based substrate.

Common industry terms for various types of laminates include:

- *High-pressure laminate (HPL)*, which refers to the conditions under which the material is formed;

- *Post-formed laminate*, which refers to material that arrives for installation with the laminate already adhered to the substrate, cut and ready to install; and
- *Through-color laminate*, which eliminates a common problem related to dark edges forming on the countertop surface.

The number of edge options, or edge profiles, is relatively limitless since the wood-based substrate can be milled to any desired profile, either by laminating edge strips or using a mitered edge.

Common manufacturer names in the laminate industry include Formica, Nevamar, VT Industries, and Wilsonart.

Concerns and Objections

Two major physical drawbacks to laminate materials exist. The first is that the laminate layer is thin, which can reduce durability. The second is the fact that the top layer is predominantly plastic, which can be inadvertently scratched, chemically etched, or burned from a hot pot, for example, causing the material to melt.

New developments in coating materials, such as aluminum oxide, for the top clear coat of the countertop have made laminate countertops somewhat more durable, but they are still easily scratched. The material can be repaired, but because laminate is thin the likelihood of damage is high. Another concern associated with laminate surfaces has to do with the edging of the material, which often shows seams and may delaminate and start to separate from the substrate over time.

Due to the chemicals and agents used in the resins for top finish coats and binding agents, there is very little that is considered environmentally friendly about laminate countertops, as they have traditionally appeared on the market. However, recent additions to the laminate countertop market, including a green substrate material, such as no-added-formaldehyde (NAF) medium-density fiberboard (MDF) have created a greener version. This altered construction introduces some sustainable attributes, while keeping the cost down, but the physical downfalls of the material remain; it still may be damaged and scratched due to the inherent performance shortcomings.

These limitations notwithstanding, laminate was very popular in the 1950s thanks to its low cost and ease of installation. Today—now that greener laminate products are finally available—projects that require a low cost, easily maintained surface may benefit from laminates formed with a formaldehyde-free substrate material.

Soid Surface

In contrast to the three-layer composition of laminates, solid surface materials refers to virtually any countertop or surfacing material composed of a single material all the way through.

However, for purposes of this discussion, we are going to limit the topic to plastic-based countertop and surfacing materials. Solid surfaces have become very popular in the last twenty or thirty years as advances in plastics technology created a durable material that is available in a multitude of colors and patterns. This alternative quickly became a popular option for bathrooms and kitchen countertops, integrated sinks, backsplashes and surrounds, as well as shower walls and shower pans. Recently, more creative applications of the versatile solid surface materials have been used for room dividers, stand-alone sinks and tops, accent walls, and a limitless array of other options subject only to the limits of designers' imaginations.

Solid surface materials are typically created from a plastic—either an acrylic or polyester resin, or some combination of the two materials. In either form, the material is poured into molds that allow for consistency throughout the material in its various alternative forms. Although the manufacturing method for solid surface products is similar regardless of whether the material used is acrylic or polyester, there are pros and cons to each.

Acrylic is more amenable to *thermoforming* (using heat and pressure to give a product its final shape) and generates less dust in the manufacturing process, which means better air quality for employees during production.

Polyester is more resistant to certain chemical compounds and allows more color depth to be observed in the material.

> *The process of **thermoforming** is used on many plastics, where sheets of material are heated until they are soft, and then shaped using molds to create a predetermined shape. The material is then cooled and trimmed back to its final shape. Thermoforming can be a lower cost method than alternative techniques, such as injection molding, which can have expensive tooling and forms. Thermoforming also allows for quicker prototype creation and ultimately faster production times.*

However, acrylic and polyester resin are quite similar—and just as their methods of fabrication are similar, so too are their overall performance. Both are durable and easy to maintain.

The benefits of a solid surface material are its uniform nature (which allows for a consistent color and texture throughout); its resistance to stains, impacts, and scratches; and the ease with which it can be cleaned. A plastic solid surface, it is highly malleable and can incorporate forms beyond the cutting of a piece of plywood. It can be bent to a radius and also thermoformed to incorporate backsplashes and various edges relatively easily. Another advantage of solid surface is that, similar to wood, solid state countertops can be fabricated with ease. Once a sheet of the material is created, it can simply be milled and cut with normal woodworking tools to fit the specific application. Most countertop

fabricators will have equipment and tooling that is needed for solid surface material fabrication at their facility, since it is a major portion of their business, and the investment in the manufacturing equipment will likely pay for itself over time.

With solid surface materials, seams are virtually invisible. Sanding the cut edges can make them impossible to differentiate from the solid sheets of material. In final form, plastic solid surface is water-resistant and does not need to be sealed. Any small scratches that do occur can be easily buffed out with an abrasive material, such as a scrubbing pad or sandpaper. The available colors and patterns for solid surface materials are quite extensive and comprehensive, with some of the materials incorporating a marbled or veined texture to mimic natural stone. While solid surface materials look similar to natural stone, the physical qualities of the plastic materials are, of course, very different. Solid surface countertops will not have the same cool feel of natural stone and they can be damaged by leaving a hot pot on them or by exposing the material to excessive heat.

Concerns and Objections

As petroleum-based plastic materials, solid surfaces would seem to be destined to the realm of non-green options. The reality, however, is that these materials can have some amount of recycled content incorporated into their compounds.

Using recycled plastic—from either pre-consumer or post-consumer material—in the manufacturing process is the best way to "green up" solid surfacing materials. Many manufacturing processes create plastic by-products, often viewed as waste, as a result of their operations. Manufacturers who take advantage of this readily available material (noted as pre-consumer recycled content in the recycling world) can create a solid surface material that can be up to 50% recycled content.

Pre-consumer Versus Post-consumer Material

Pre-consumer material is material that has not been put into finished form and is likely a byproduct or waste product from the extraction and manufacturing process. Metal shavings from a steel mill that have been left on the mill floor qualify as pre-consumer material.

Post-consumer material, on the other hand, is material that has been out in the market place, used by a consumer, and has reached the end of its useful life. A plastic beverage bottle that someone has left after drinking its contents is a post-consumer material.

The primary issue with green options for solid surface products currently available from major U.S. manufacturers is the somewhat constrained color palette. This problem arises because manufacturers do not have extensive control over the pre-consumer waste material that's generated, so they may end up with mixed colors to incorporate into their feedstock mix. In addition, the colors resulting from the recycled content can be bland and drab.

Some solid surface manufacturers have access to a more refined recycling system, particularly in many European countries where product recycling is widespread and the process more mature. Over seventy vibrant colors, all incorporating recycled content, are available from these producers.

When evaluating recycled content, another important factor you should consider is the source of the recycled materials. Are they scraps from the manufacturer's existing processes that are simply built back into their own processes, or are they scraps actually being diverted from the recycling stream? Companies that actually divert waste from the landfill, rather than simply managing the waste they create themselves, are making a larger contribution to sustainability through their efforts.

The most common types of plastic-based solid surfacing materials on the market are familiar names such as Corian, Avonite, and Durat.
Corian: *www.corian.com*
Avonite: *www.Avonitesurfaces.com*
Durat: *www.durat.com*

Granite, Marble, and Natural Stone

Increasingly popular over the last two decades, natural stone has emerged as a hallmark of countertop luxury. Granite, limestone, marble, slate, and a variety of other mined stones are extracted as large stones and later cut into slabs. These slabs are further cut and polished to create the elegant countertops that can be found in many high-end spaces in a variety of architectural and interior design styles.

Granite is the most popular choice for natural stone countertops. Available in a range of grades from low to high, the differing degrees of quality will, of course, result in significant price variations for consumers. Marble is another natural stone option, but it is softer than granite and more porous. These differences make marble more susceptible to staining as well as more easily damaged or etched by chemicals. Limestone and travertine are similar in performance to marble, as they are also softer and porous. All three—marble, limestone, and travertine—are typically quite expensive and as with all natural stones—including granite—must be sealed periodically.

Concerns and Objections

As with all natural products, some inherent color variation and veining occurs due to the minerals forming in the earth for hundreds of years. Some will consider this part of the beauty of the natural material; others may find too great a variation unacceptable.

Quarries in North America produce granite, limestone, and travertine as well as some other types of building stone. While North American quarries do serve a segment of the market for natural stone countertops, the bulk of the material comes from overseas countries, many in Asia, thus adding appreciably to freight costs and the carbon footprint of these materials.

Beyond the physical considerations of the material itself, a number of peripheral and associated concerns need to be considered during material selection. The primary concern with natural stone is the mining and labor practices within the mines. The ecosystems surrounding the mines can suffer seriously. Pollution and contamination due to storm water runoff, clear-cutting forests and growth for truck routes, and errant or mismanaged construction debris can all be detrimental to certain areas. While these factors don't seem directly related at first glance, they are all highly important to consider when selecting materials.

A prevalent misconception regarding natural stone is that because it is naturally occurring, it is somehow an infinite resource. Nothing could be further from the truth. Natural stone is decidedly finite, having taken centuries, even millennia, to form. From this perspective, it's clear that we cannot continue to mine stone and have it remain plentiful. The issue is essentially the same as harvesting old-growth forests and demands that we pay attention to the long-term impacts and depletion that result from mining this resource.

A third issue that arises when using stone is the transportation and processing needed to transform it from to embedded form in the ground to its installation as a sophisticated, installed countertop. Stone is inherently heavy and the material is extracted, shipped, and fabricated in slabs. The result is a very energy-intensive process, which, as we mentioned, can leave a sizable carbon footprint in relation to the amount of material provided. If you use natural stone, the best option is to try to find stone that has been mined and manufactured as close to the project location as possible, minimizing the energy expenditure to the greatest extent possible. This approach may also cut the cost significantly.

Engineered Stone

An alternative to solid natural stone is engineered stone. This hybrid approach combines the benefits of plastic-based solid surface materials (described earlier) and stone chips. Engineered stone material is made of about 90% stone chips, typically quartz. The chips are combined with resin and formed into sheets for countertops or other surfacing applications. Since this material is man-made, it is not as dependent on mining the large slabs of stone that are typically needed.

Granite is typically composed of 40–60% quartz, the material that gives granite its hardness and durability. Quartz is also what causes engineered stone to be more durable than its natural counterpart.

Engineered stone can provide visual uniformity whereas natural stone is subject to many naturally occurring variations that cannot be controlled. Engineered stone also offers considerable flexibility in the look and composition of countertops, contingent on both the size and type of aggregates used in the manufacturing process, as well as the color pigments. The manufacturer can vary these two factors in order to alter the appearance of the final product, giving consumers the durability of natural stone with the increased flexibility in color and style of an engineered material.

Resin also enhances the stain and bacterial resistance of the surface compared to natural stone, which is porous and more likely to absorb foreign elements. Engineered stone does not need to be sealed, is easy to clean, and nonporous.

Any stone fabricator that can cut natural stone should also be able to cut engineered stone. The manipulation of the finished material is not an issue in the construction process.

Concerns and Objections

As we have mentioned numerous times, using local materials is your best option. However, when it comes to engineered stone in which the whole process typically does not occur within close proximity to a project site, other considerations must be examined. Stones and resins can be made from recycled content, taken from pre-consumer plastics or stone. Overall the durability and long lifetime of engineered stone for countertops are positive characteristics, provided the owner does not make a style decision that will be quickly outdated, leading to the ending up in a landfill far sooner than its functional (as distinct from its aesthetic/stylistic) lifespan would dictate. The life cycle assessment described in Chapter 4 speaks to this concern.

Using stone chips instead of slabs is, arguably, a greener choice, but only if the mining practices under industry scrutiny are avoided (see the sidebar). In all likelihood, quartz is mined similarly to natural stone and then ground into smaller sizes to create engineered stone.

As you can see, understand the manufacturing practices and know the original sources of the material components before you assume the final material product is truly a sustainable one. That said, engineered stone is moving in that direction, striving to incorporate more and more sustainably-oriented attributes.

Innovative versions of engineered stone materials have come on the market in recent years that use recycled stone, ceramic, and other materials in a resin binder, resulting in up to 75% recycled content (keep in mind that color may vary with recycled materials).

Mining Practices

Issues related to mining include erosion, soil and groundwater contamination related to chemicals released into the ecosystem by the mining processes, and biodiversity loss. Often, additional areas are cleared surrounding mines in order to make room for storing mining soil and debris. Local residents in mining areas are often affected by the contamination of the surrounding environment.

Mining can harm plants and water bodies and potentially displace wildlife populations as areas surrounding quarries are cleared to accommodate the infrastructure required to build the operations necessary to support a mine. Safety issues are another mining concern. Much mining occurs below the earth's surface and gases, such as methane and carbon monoxide, can leak into mine shafts if the ventilation is inadequate. Other illnesses such as miner's lung, silicosis, and asbestosis can be caused by dust and poor air circulation in mines.

Mining is largely unregulated, or self-regulated, and there is a great deal of longstanding popular sentiment that these processes lack sufficient oversight. The certification of mines and good practices is conducted by the International Organization for Standardization (ISO) using processes such as ISO 9000 and ISO 14001. This organization recognizes that mines have an auditable environmental management system and conducts short inspections of the mining companies and their practices. Another initiative, the Ceres' Global Reporting Initiative, offers voluntary certification, but these are not verified.

It's worth noting that these new versions take engineered stone one step further along the sustainable curve by using corn-based resins rather than the typical petroleum-based options that for so long have been the standard in engineered stone. By using corn-based resins, manufacturers are demonstrating a shift of emphasis to the binding agent rather than simply addressing stone origin and content through their shift to recycled chips.

Poured Concrete

Another increasingly popular look in countertops is poured concrete, a very versatile material. It can be a polished or given matte finish, tinted in a variety of colors, and poured in place for a seamless installation or installed in slab form just off the truck.

Concrete, as discussed in a broader sense in Chapter 5, uses a mix containing aggregate, water, and Portland cement. The material must cure and dry in order to set and form. Polished or not, the finished look is a modern, high-tech countertop that works well in many residential or commercial settings.

A recent addition to concrete countertops is the inclusion of interesting new aggregates including stone chips, porcelain, and most popular, glass chips. These add-ins expand the aesthetic options available in terms of look, feel, style, and color.

The glass aggregate is perhaps the most striking, as the mix can be tailored to form a tinted base color with a clear mixture of glass, or a mixed color palette incorporating browns,

greens, and blues. Several vendors have introduced slabs of the glass and concrete material, including Meld in Raleigh, North Carolina; IceStone in Brooklyn, New York; and Vetrazzo in California. Meld also offers poured-in-place custom installations of the glass and concrete material, such as countertops with integrated sinks, standalone sinks, and vanity tops.

The major environmental benefit of these concrete options is the fact that the glass is recycled from the waste stream, both pre- and post-consumer. In some cases, post-consumer glass from beer, wine, soda, juice, or water bottles is used. This provides a beautiful countertop that also makes a visible contribution towards and statement about sustainability.

The concrete material itself, in the case of the vendors above, often incorporates some fly ash content. Recall from the discussion in Chapter 5 that the inclusion of fly ash limits the amount of Portland cement required. Because Portland cement has a high embodied energy, minimizing the amount used in concrete by incorporating fly ash can both contribute to recycled content and have a positive environmental impact.

Due to the weight of concrete, it is best to find a material that is available close to the project site, minimizing embodied energy, transportation distance, and, of course, cost.

Concerns and Objections

While concrete serves as a mainstay in structural systems, it has also found a niche as a countertop material. Both applications share the same concerns: primarily that concrete is bulky, heavy, and takes substantial time to cure and dry.

The sheer weight of the material must be considered when using it as a countertop, as there must be sufficient structure within the cabinets below to successfully support the mass of the countertop slabs or the poured material. As mentioned earlier using fly ash and recycled decorative aggregates into countertop applications are "green" steps that will help to mitigate some of the concerns related to concrete.

Stainless Steel

Industrial and commercial kitchens are the most common venues for stainless steel countertops because the material is durable, relatively light, easily formed, and easily cleaned. The material is also anti-bacterial and will not stain, hence the name. For all of these reasons, stainless steel is an excellent material for use in a food preparation area.

Unfortunately, stainless steel scratches relatively easily, so it may not be desirable for mainstream residential applications, although it will certainly make a great countertop in a kitchen that has similar requirements to those described above, or where the owner wants the sleek, clean, industrial look of stainless steel.

For a discussion of the extraction, manufacturing, and finishing processes of stainless steel and other pertinent information refer back to the detailed discussion of steel in Chapter 5. Do remember that the material is easily recycled, so using high-recycled content steel is a good choice if stainless steel is in your material palette.

Concerns and Objections

As with concrete, steel has broader—and more popular—structural applications. Relatively speaking, the amount of steel used in countertops is a very small portion of overall steel use, though it is certainly a viable possibility in some situations. For a review of environmental concerns related to the procurement of steel, revisit Chapter 5. When it comes to using steel in a countertop application as noted, fingerprints, dents, and scratching can occur. While stainless steel countertops are absolutely durable, they're not going to retain the pristine look of other countertop choices that don't dent or show scratches and fingerprints as readily as stainless steel does.

Butcher Block and Agrifiber

Beyond the usual array of countertop options just discussed, an increasing number of new material options have emerged. Unlike the other countertop materials, these new materials have entered the market from the get-go as sustainable options.

Wood-based countertops, typically called butcher block, are strips or cubes of material laminated together to form a solid countertop piece. Butcher block countertops can be made from any variety of wood, including walnut, hard maple, ash, or beech. If you refer back to earlier chapters that delve more deeply into choosing sustainable wood options (see Chapter 7 on wood flooring, for example), you'll find sustainably harvested or reclaimed woods that can be used to create beautiful, natural wood-based countertops. Bamboo can also be used in a butcher block countertop.

Agrifiber-based materials—such as paper-based, sunflower seed hulls, straw, and wheat boards—can be processed to make them durable enough to perform as a surfacing material for countertops. Paper-based countertops are very common and can be found in many industrial applications under the brand names Paperstone and Richlite.

Concerns and Objections

The same general environmental concerns for procuring wood for structural and flooring applications apply to wood-based countertops. With agrifiber materials, the primary concerns are related to the durability, porosity, and water resistance of the countertop. The finish used on agrifiber products can enhance the durability; however, you will want to make sure that the finish itself is also environmentally accountable.

Summary

Countertops, covering an integral and often communal surface area in the home or office, can be one of the most important features in designing and finishing a space.

In addition to the look and feel of a countertop, the material(s) from which it is made and the original source of those materials are important concerns in making an appropriate and sustainable selection. Stone products are durable, but the techniques and practices used to get them into your home may not align with the sustainability profile you had in mind. While laminate countertops have dominated the market in the past, they can often use many undesirable components in their composition, from the base wood core to the adhesives used in the laminate. Every countertop option has benefits and drawbacks, and many manufacturers are now incorporating more sustainable practices into their existing lines of countertop and surfacing options. With the addition of new materials designed specifically to be green from the outset, our sustainable choices for countertops are growing.

Chapter 9: Millwork—Casework, Wall Paneling, and Trim

When the construction process progresses through the structural and envelope layers of the project, work can commence on the major interior elements. Another significant aspect of an interior with green material options is millwork.

Millwork refers to any woodwork, including doors, window casings, and baseboards, that have been machined by a lumber mill. Built-in cabinetry, door or window trims, moldings at ceiling or chair-rail height, wall paneling, and wainscoting are also considered millwork. Essentially, any wood or wood composite that has been refined from its raw state of fresh-cut lumber and milled fall within this rubric. In fact, much of the millwork in buildings is built-in, secured in place rather than applied to a surface later (as would be done with paint or carpeting). Making decisions about millwork is a critical step before considering other applied finishes.

Millwork pieces can be sourced as sheet goods or dimensional pieces, both of which can be purchased in larger sizes and trimmed on site as needed. Sheet goods are commonly sized at 4x8 feet and at various degrees of thickness. Material options in sheet goods generally include Agrifiber, medium-density fiberboard (MDF), composite boards, oriented strand board (OSB), particle board, and plywood.

Dimensional lumber is simply another size category, typically available in a wider variety of lengths and widths expressed in inches. The most familiar is, of course, the ever-popular 2x4 commonly found in wood construction in the U.S. As we mentioned when discussing framing lumber in Chapter 6, the dimensions are given as 2x4, however the actual dimensions of the lumber are thinner due to the milling process. Dimensional lumber is available in a choice of hardwoods and softwoods.

While a number of PVC-based "wood-like" plastics are used in trim applications, this chapter focuses primarily on the millwork issues, concerns, and possibilities related to wood and wood-derived products, not wood substitutes. In the following sections we will take a look at the composition of many millwork products, as well as their primary advantages and disadvantages and the trends within the wood industry.

Composition
Wood

Wood is a natural resource that typically requires or uses very little processing compared to other building materials. For example, the extraction and manufacturing process for metals involves the energy-intensive removal of ore from a mine of some sort, followed by a series of refining and manufacturing processes that may include: washing to prepare the material; smelting to reduce the ore to a workable liquid; liquation, to separate different metals at different melting points; or distillation, which sends some metals into vapor at a certain temperature, which are then condensed to a liquid or solid. These are only a few of the many processes undertaken to create a usable metal material suitable for building applications. With wood, however, you cut it down at the site—without digging extensively into the earth—and then cut the lumber to appropriate pieces in a mill. Overall, the general process is much less complicated than for metals and has been going on for centuries.

Wood can be worked with in any of its many forms, dimensional lumber, strips, chips, wood pulp, and dust being the most popular. Based on the form of the starting material, the wood may be cut into dimensional lumber for trim, formed into sheets, or extruded into trim pieces of various shapes and

Agrifiber: A composite board composed primarily of compressed agricultural fibers such as wheat board.

Composite Boards: An engineered composite product that includes not only particles of wood, but also other elements, possibly plastic or recycled, to increase the stability and strength of the board.

Oriented Strand Board (OSB): A wood product that is performance-rated and designed for strength. Strands of wood are layered in strategic orientations and sealed with an adhesive; the directionality of the wood strands as well as the binder material increases the strength of the material.

Particle Board: An engineered wood product manufactured from a variety of wood particles, such as chips, shavings, and sawdust. The material uses a binder, like a synthetic resin or similar adhesive, to secure the wood particles and provide added strength.

Plywood: A material created by gluing or cementing sheets of wood together; the direction of the grains in adjacent layers are positioned at a wide or right angle.

sizes and then painted, sealed, or stained to achieve a particular look. Such applications typically use softwoods, traditionally fir, spruce, and pine.

Dimensional cuts are frequently given priority in the mill as they are the primary use of the starting lumber. However, the residual strips, chips, and dust can be just as useful in creating wood products that are in demand, and allow for an efficient use of what would otherwise be waste material. A number of wood products actually rely primarily on these post-industrial scraps, making use of as much of the raw wood material as possible.

As discussed in Chapter 7, hardwoods are typically used for high-wear flooring due to their durability. However, these hardwoods may also be used for millwork, and while the alternatives for hardwood millwork are the same as those for hardwood flooring, there are other options as well for millwork sheet goods. We've already addressed the sustainability requirements for wood in the realms of structure and flooring, so let's to expand the realm of wood alternatives as seen in the millwork market.

Bamboo and Palmwood

Rugged grasses (e.g., bamboo and palmwood) are popular green alternatives to wood, not just for flooring, but also for millwork. Both of these rugged grasses have extremely impressive tensile strength, making them very hard and very durable.

Technically categorized as a woody perennial evergreen, bamboo is one of the fastest-growing woody plants in the world—in some places they can grow to nearly 48" in one day![48] Palmwood typically comes from old coconut palm plantations where the trees no longer have the ability to bear fruit, amounting to millions of coconut trees felled in the tropics each year.

Many of these rugged grasses, particularly bamboo, are viewed as invasive plants that need to be watched carefully. Because bamboo grows so quickly, it is considered rapidly renewable (i.e. it can be harvested within ten years or less). Bamboo is ready for use in construction in as few as three to seven years in contrast with some hardwoods or old growth tree types that may take nearly one hundred years to reach maturity. Palmwood, on the other hand, is harvested after the tree has been bearing fruit for over seventy years. While its growth cycle is not considered rapidly renewable, the amount of trees "expiring" each year is thought to be sufficient to assure availability of this material.

Bamboo is used to form plywood sheets when milled from its original grass form. The exterior walls of the grass, which are over an inch thick, are cut into strips. These strips are then laminated together to form solid or plywood sheets that are used in lieu of conventional plywood. Like bamboo, palmwood, can be milled from the thick, fibrous walls of the plants into sheet goods for use in millwork.

Most bamboo and palmwood comes from Asia, where the environmental conditions are suitable to their growth. The bamboo commonly found in American backyards is not the same bamboo used for millwork. Attempts are underway to establish local sources in the U.S. for the same varieties of bamboo that yield construction-grade material. However, the climatic conditions and harvesting capabilities must be conducive for the plants to achieve the growth characteristics necessary for use in millwork applications.

Agrifiber

Manufactured using biofiber from crops, plants, or grass, agrifiber is a rapidly developing alternative to wood in the construction industry. Each type of agrifiber is typically renewed on a yearly basis by the fresh growth of a specific crop which may be wheat, straw, sorghum, sunflower, or even rice. These byproduct fibers are bonded with an adhesive or resins to create panels of composite boards with a uniform material throughout (such as strawboard or wheatboard), and used in lieu of an MDF panel or OSB in varying thicknesses. Or, the fibers can be formed into a three- or five-ply board in varying thicknesses (as is the case with Kirei, or sorghum board). Depending on the specific composition and the base material used, agrifiber products provide varying levels of structural integrity.

Paper

Wood by-products such as paper or wood pulp can also be used to form paneling or other millwork applications. Several sheet goods on the market (e.g., Paperstone, Richlite, and Eco-Top) are the by-product of wood pulp or recycled paper, resins, and some coloring agents manufactured into panels of various thicknesses. The amount of recycled content and composition of each varies based on the source of the materials

and manufacturing processes. EcoTop, for example, also contains bamboo. (Specifics can be found on the individual manufacturers' websites.)

While genuine wood elements can hold their own once they are cut into boards or panels, a binding agent, usually resin, is needed for the composite materials together, and adhesives are needed for the creation of plywood. Various resins—each with their own primary ingredients and concerns—may also function as adhesives in plywood materials. More will be said about these concerns in the next section.

Concerns and Objections

As with all material selections, various issues arise when selecting millwork products that meet sustainability criteria. As indicated in the discussion of wood flooring in Chapter 7, the issues aren't always about the wood itself. Let's take a closer look.

Material Origin and Transportation Issues

It is possible to cut down so much wood it will not be able to regenerate fast enough to support current construction rates and maintain the forest habitat and ecosystems. Reports of clear-cutting rainforests and losing hardwoods at a rate that will take hundreds of years to replenish reminds us of this fact. The harvesting practices of different types of wood crops and how well each crop is managed are at the heart of this issue.

Noted organizations, such as FSC and the SFI, verify and certify individual forests as well-managed and producing environmentally responsible products. Some of these options are reviewed below in the Alternatives section.

However, some sustainability experts believe that no matter how well managed forests are, the available supplies of wood around the world will not be sufficient to meet the increased demand for wood of all kinds. Similarly, if the quality of soil is damaged in some locations to the point that it cannot grow trees, or the water level rises and takes over forested land, there could, in fact, be a wood shortage. These issues and potential circumstances would, ultimately, make wood a finite resource, at least for the next few generations until systems can either rebalance themselves or adapt accordingly.

While wood tends to be perceived as a natural resource a variety of wood composite materials including wood scraps and remnants can be engineered to help reduce our dependence on hardwoods. Since some engineered woods come from overseas, an important question becomes the location of manufactured material. The wood is not simply being felled in a forest but processed into a final form, where this processing occurs and what is involved in transporting the material from initial harvesting through each step in the manufacturing process all become questions of sustainability. How does the material get from the source to the manufacturing location and, ultimately, to the project site where it will be used?

It is not uncommon to have several intermediaries touching or reforming the material—both natural and manufactured—along the way, making this chain of custody potentially long and complicated.

As we said at the start of the book, the LEED Rating System gives credit for regional materials, sourced and manufactured within a 500-mile radius. This sounds simple enough, but the credits are subdivided further to pinpoint where the material is extracted, where it is processed, and where it is manufactured. It is not just a question of where the forest itself is located, but also where the wood may stop off en route to the final project site. As discussed in earlier chapters, this issue is fundamentally one of embodied energy, and how much is expended while transporting the material from wherever it was "born" to the project site. Put another way, it is not enough to say that the wood was harvested from a forest in Virginia. If it is an engineered piece of wood, it is also important to understand where the engineering of the lumber took place. Much of the engineered lumber stock in the U.S. comes from overseas; that added transportation impact is of concern in sustainability discussions.

To understand why, start by imagining that the initial wood stock lumber comes from a forest in Virginia, is transported to a port in New Orleans, and shipped overseas to China. The product is received at a port in China and from there, shipped to a mill that engineers the lumber into sheet goods. Then the newly formed sheets are put back on a ship out of China and transported back to the port in New Orleans. Finally, the engineered product is shipped to the job site ten miles down the road from the forest in Virginia where it was originally harvested. This illustrates a circuitous but sadly not unrealistic route—one that entirely violates the intent of using regional materials. You must consider the route the product has traveled in order to understand just how sustainable the millwork you are considering will be in your application.

Formaldehyde

Binding resins are an integral component of engineered wood, much of which is used for millwork. Resins containing formaldehyde may be plant-, water-, or petroleum-based; or contain phenolic resins phenol formaldehyde and urea formaldehyde. As we said earlier in the book, though formaldehyde is one of the most popular binding resins used in engineered products because of its availability, cost-effectiveness, and good performance characteristics, it has many drawbacks as well. In higher concentrations, formaldehyde and urea formaldehyde (UF) are carcinogenetic substances, and have been cited by the EPA for potentially dangerous side-effects.[49] Formaldehyde's widespread and unregulated use in some foreign countries well-known for low-cost manufacturing makes control over these substances a primary concern in building materials that come from these sources and locations.

Finishes, Coatings, and Volatile Organic Compounds (VOCs)

Another consideration and concern regarding the use of millwork are the finishes applied to the woods or wood composites themselves. Although wood millwork items are sometimes installed in their raw form, it is more likely that a coating of some sort will be applied in the form of a finish, clear coat, stain, or paint. While these will be addressed more fully in Chapter 11 on finishes, suffice it to say here that it is possible that by using a pungent coating, you may run the risk of transforming an initially harmless millwork installation into a causal factor in occupant headaches and nausea.

Alternatives/Best Choices

In response to marketplace concerns about wood sourcing, finishing, and installation, a number of product evolutions and alternatives that provide greener options have emerged. The products listed below respond to the concerns we've outlined earlier and represent the best options currently available on the market. As with everything in the green movement, products and processes are rapidly changing, so be sure to do your own research and choose the materials with which you are most comfortable after weighing cost, durability, performance, and sustainability criteria. Remember that the FSC is the certification of choice for finding a green wood product to use in your millwork, although methodologies and certification criteria from other groups are currently being considered.

NAF (No-Added Formaldehyde) or Formaldehyde-Free Boards

A number of new products hitting the market use no-added formaldehyde (NAF) or no-added urea formaldehyde (NAUF) to fill the demand for healthy woods with environmentally friendly alternatives. For example, in April 2007, the California Air Resources Board (CARB) implemented an Airborne Toxic Control Measure (ATCM) to decrease formaldehyde emissions from composite wood products including hardwood, plywood, medium-density fiberboard, and particle board. ATCM requires either a third-party certifier for composite wood products or the use of NAF resin as a replacement.[50] NAF composite boards are quickly becoming a viable and cost-appropriate alternative. Nearly all composite boards are now available with an NAF option. Costs have come down substantially with the increased competition for market share among most mainstream manufacturers.

Rapidly Renewable Products

Fundamentally, the use of rapidly renewable materials will prevent your project from contributing to deforestation, as these materials should cycle from seed to maturity more quickly than the products will be needed in the marketplace. A significant number of rapidly renewable materials that perform as well as traditional wood products are available on the market. The rugged grasses described earlier in this chapter are one of the more popular alternatives to traditionally harvested wood species found in the U.S. Bamboo, cork, and palmwood are the most common, particularly because they provide quick turnaround in maturity

Unfortunately, most of these popular, rapidly renewable plants, like bamboo, cork, and palmwood, are not native to North America. For this reason, you must carefully weigh the benefits of using a rapidly renewable product against a more local material to determine which makes the most sense for your project.

Reclaimed Woods/Recycled Content Products

Reclaimed or salvaged wood is another option to consider for your millwork needs. Whether the wood product has been used previously in a building application—perhaps as a door, or flooring, or trim or cabinetry—there is the possibility that the old product can find a new home in a new project.

Demand has similarly increased for reclaimed boards, such as those taken from old barns or industrial buildings. Disassembled from barns, wide plank boards, huge wood beams, and hand-hewn beams are available at traditional sizes unavailable in lumber yards today. This type of old, recycled lumber is also a dry wood, as opposed to recently felled wood, which ultimately means that it is less likely to warp or become disfigured. There are even businesses that pull old lumber from the bottom of rivers and lake beds and mill them down for reuse. These types of wood products lighten the demand on forest production and provide a character for spaces that cannot easily be found with the traditional wood harvesting process.

Reclaimed woods are one of the best options for sourcing quality wood products, capitalizing on the sustainability angle in the process. The industry surrounding the reclamation of building materials continues to prosper, with reclaimed wood leading the way as deconstruction companies focus on pulling as much reusable material as possible from existing buildings.

The increased viability of this business will result in more varieties, sizes, and volumes of reclaimed wood and will push the price point down to a level competitive with fresh-cut lumber. Reclaimed wood was explored earlier in the flooring chapter, an application that is likely to make more use of the wide availability of hardwoods from existing buildings, as durability is a much more stringent consideration for flooring applications. Millwork is often stained or painted, which would not necessarily warrant the use of a reclaimed material, especially if the character of the wood is not a consideration. When solid hardwood is being considered for millwork, however, reclaimed wood is an excellent option.

It is important to note the distinction between reclaimed wood and recycled content. While it may seem that reclaimed wood immediately falls into the category of recycled material, this is not necessarily the case. If wood is taken from an existing building and has already been milled (for example, in the form of a door or molding), it could contribute to the recycled content credit found in many rating systems. However, if a log is reclaimed from the bottom of a river, it has not yet been milled has not entered the manufacturing stream—and therefore cannot be considered recycled. In this case, the log would be considered to a local material instead. One useful way to think of the distinction is that a material is considered reclaimed if it has been "re-purposed" from its original application.

Recycled Content in Composite Boards

If your millwork needs can be met by using a composite board, using a board with the highest amount of recycled content is obviously the best choice. Scraps on the mill floor can be used to make composite boards (pre-consumer recycled content), making it a very low energy option. Also because the manufacturing of composite board is a low-cost process to begin with, the price premium for boards with recycled content is not an inhibiting factor.

Other building materials—aluminum and steel, for example—often contain high levels of recycled content. Although it is still preferable to use them over harvesting new resources, they are often a high energy option due to the recycling process. In the case of aluminum cans, they have already been manufactured and have to be broken down again to be used as recycled material. This requires two complete and additional processes: an initial process to break down the cans and another to reform the material into a new recycled product.

Composite Boards with Non-finite Resources

Similar to the composite board options already outlined, other composite board products are available that are made of non-finite materials, also referred to as bio-based materials, which can be considered rapidly renewable. These materials are often agricultural fibers such as sunflower hulls, wheat or straw, sorghum, and even recycled newsprint and paper fibers. Some of these products are engineered with layers of resin and fibers, creating a board that is even stronger than traditional plywood. Other boards have a uniform look similar to MDF, with a resin used as a binding agent between the bio-based materials. This creates an aesthetic different from the layered look of a plywood product. The bio-based boards can be used in an unfinished form and have a unique, organic look. Some alternative boards can be stained depending on the starting material and its ability to absorb a staining agent. An emerging trend in composite boards is the introduction of water-based polymers and dyes that reinforce the durability of the boards and give composites a finished look more suitable for wall paneling and cabinetry.

Regional Wood Materials

As we've said all along, the benefits of specifying local materials are multidimensional. Less energy is spent in its transportation, for one. You must consider where the material is harvested (extracted), processed, manufactured, and installed in order to truly assess a product's energy expenditure, but with wood this process is fairly straightforward.

Another benefit to using local material is the contribution you make to main street movements and "mom and pop" businesses. Whether or not the lumber business down the street is a "mom and pop" shop, it is definitely contributing to the local economy and livelihood of the surrounding community. Sustainability starts at the local level, so specifying local materials is always a good alternative. That said, it is critical to assess the regional content of the material in conjunction with its harvesting practices. If mom and pop are clear cutting to secure their lumber selection, it may not be the most sustainable option.

Trends and Evolution

As we've shown in this chapter, when selecting a wood material for millwork—or any other use—you may well face a choice between using reclaimed wood, regional wood products, or FSC certified products. Depending on budgetary consideration, time, and logistics, one choice might make more sense over another. For example, while lumber may be plentiful in states like North Carolina and Arkansas, it is very difficult (if not impossible) to find FSC certified lumber within the 500-mile radius defined by LEED in Arizona. Understanding that the LEED rating system and other rating systems like it are constantly evolving, this logistical snare may not be an issue for long, but it is worth considering as you investigate your options.

All in all, you have a number of valid opportunities for greening up your millwork and casework in any project—and new options are constantly being introduced. From rapidly renewable materials like bamboo, wheat, straw, palmwood, paper, sunflower, and other plant fibers, to those that are recycled, reclaimed, or salvaged, the demand and ingenuity of greener products is definitely on the rise.

Chapter 10: Furniture

Now that we have made our way through the different material components you need to consider when thinking green, we will address the final touches to nearly any space—the furniture. Discussing furniture from a green perspective can get a bit tricky because depending on the type of furniture any number of the material components previously reviewed could be present in its construction. Wood, stain, fabric, steel—you name it. So in this chapter, we'll tackle the discussion in a slightly different way than we have in previous chapters. We'll address the various material components you're likely to encounter in your search for "green furniture" and refer you to relevant sections of the book where appropriate. In addition to talking about the different physical and compositional aspects of sustainable furniture, we will describe some resources available in the search for sustainable furnishings, review some concerns that merit your attention during the selection process, discuss possible alternatives and better choices that are available in the market right now, and high-

light some trends we anticipate will be coming in the near future.

The sustainability considerations for furniture bring together all of the concepts we've covered thus far from raw materials and chemical considerations to life cycle issues. Consumers are increasingly concerned about making smart environmental choices related to the materials and off-gassing of their furnishings. However, a much larger movement and rapidly growing market centers on sustainable commercial office furniture because it's here where the market is so enormous—cost considerations are paramount and turnover is high, leading to an abundance of used furniture, much of which ends up in the landfill.

In an effort to drastically reduce the impact of business furniture on the environment, the Business and Institutional Furniture Manufacturer's Association (BIFMA) developed the Furniture Sustainability Standard (BIFMA E3-2008). This standard is divided into four basic elements consisting of various prerequisites and credits, similar to the rating systems and certifications we talked about earlier. The four basic elements are: (1) materials, (2) energy and atmosphere, (3) human and ecosystem health, and (4) social responsibility. Several government organizations, universities, corporations, and green building rating systems have adopted all or part of the BIFMA Furniture Sustainability Standard.

Intelligent design (also referred to as design for environment) is a concept that is central to sustainability in furniture, particuarly office furniture. This concept refers to a variety of design approaches, all of which attempt to reduce the overall environmental impact of a specific product, including the environmental impacts of the processes to create, transport, and dispose of that product throughout its life cycle. One approach is cradle to cradle, which works holistically to redesign entire systems. With intelligent design, careful raw material selection involves considering recycled content, rapidly renewable materials, and certified wood. Thinking beyond the manufacturing of the product, intelligent design also considers designing for reduced packaging, durability, reuse, and disassembly. In other words, making furniture that can be easily taken apart and fixed or recycled. We also expect to see governments and rating systems begin to require buy-back or take-back programs, as the carpet industry has already begun to implement, where the manufacturer accepts responsibility for the product throughout its life, including taking the product back from the customer at the end of its useful life for recycling or reuse. In this arrangement, the consumer is effectively leasing the furniture from the manufacturer who will have to deal with the disposal or refurnishing of the piece.

Composition

Having already devoted considerable time to the topic of wood, we will be brief in our discussion of it here. Wood can be incorporated into furniture in any number of ways, whether it is visible on the exterior or not. Perhaps more than any other use, natural wood used in furniture can achieve some pretty remarkable aesthetics, for example, the beautiful arms of a chair or to create a sophisticated, sculpted table. However, the material composition of the wood, no matter how it is used, is just as important when we are thinking about environmental impacts. For more in depth information on considerations regarding wood, refer to Chapter 7 on Flooring.

One of the more common areas where wood is used in furnishings, but not often seen, is in shelving and drawer boxes, or unexposed areas of standalone cabinets, dressers, and tables. Because these areas are often underexposed, using more costly solid woods would not necessarily make sense. Inexpensive structural components such as plywood, particle board, or MDF can help keep costs down. Before purchasing furniture, which uses these more economical boards, refer to the criteria presented in previous chapters pertaining to the use of engineered wood. Look for products with minimal formaldehyde, or products that incorporate recycled content, and/or selecting woods that are sustainably harvested.

Veneers are also common in furniture. While they provide a cost-effective alternative to solid woods, veneers can affect durability if they are damaged and the cheaper structural material below is exposed.

Veneers are often made from plastic-based laminates that look like wood, but which raise the same concerns about furniture that were outlined with respect to laminate countertops and other petroleum-based products. These petroleum-based products can be found in couches, chairs, desks, tables, and even systems furniture. Veneers may also be laminated to a substrate using an adhesive that off gasses. Given this, the sustainable choices when it comes to veneers are those produced from sustainably harvested materials (typically FSC)— or reconstituted or recycled wood pulp or other organic material—and then affixed with low-VOC or zero-VOC adhesives and glues.

Another consideration associated primarily with furniture is the issue of off-gassing from the foam and padding used for comfort or fabric-wrapped panels in systems furniture. As with many types of synthetic foams and materials, the padding product is typically exposed to a number of chemical agents during its production and refinement. The issue of off-gassing in synthetic foams is of widespread concern, for example, in mattresses where extended exposure to some emissions has been known to cause reactions in people with chemical sensitivities. A related concern for synthetic pads is that many are petroleum-based and, therefore, contribute to CO_2 production. An obvious answer to this would be to select natural foam or padding when available. However, the base material is often not the only issue; many treatments used on furnishings are in response to fire-retardant requirements found in building and occupant codes. Even natural materials may be subject to these same fire-retardant treatments.

In line with this theme of off-gassing and emissions from furniture materials is the issue of flame-retardant fabrics. Like many topics in green building, this use is contested. The Consumer Product Safety Commission (CPSC)[51] maintains that substances commonly found in fire-retardant chemicals (such as vinyl chloride and boric acid) do not pose a health risk to users.[52] On the other hand, the U.S. Public Interest Research Group (U.S. PIRG) cites research linking flame retardants to cancer, asthma, and liver damage.[53] One option for protection against these potentially harmful chemicals is to use vinyl-covered foams and mattresses, allowing the vinyl to become the barrier between the chemicals and the user. Unfortunately, vinyl comes with its own set of environmental issues and contradictions. As we have mentioned throughout the book, there are often tradeoffs that must be weighed to determine which factors are most critical to the end user. Luckily, regardless of who is right or wrong in the discussion surrounding fire-retardant chemicals, a number of alternative fabrics and foams on the market are untreated and in a close-to-natural state. These include organic cottons or wools, which are both rapidly renewable and healthy, if safely grown and harvested.

Another area of concern for fabrics is that many soft goods are treated with formaldehyde, the same substance discussed in Chapter 9 in regard to composite wood products, which can contribute to nausea and breathing difficulties among other health concerns. The best way to limit or eliminate exposure to formaldehyde is to use organic or non-treated fabrics and air out the furniture as much as possible before using it regularly. Fabrics are often not thought of as a permanent part of designs, but do contribute significantly to indoor air quality.

Additional considerations for fabrics in furniture and draperies include the distinction between organic cotton and other organic textiles. Organic cotton fabrics ensure that the cotton fibers themselves were raised and harvested with sustainability in mind; organic textile labels guarantee that the entire process of fabric manufacturing (including water use, chemicals, energy, dyes, finishing, etc.) was treated and executed with as much care. Fabric certifications are available from organizations such as Green Guard, Cradle to Cradle, and The Global Organic Textiles Standard. These various certifications may address carbon footprinting, social aspects of the textile manufacturing, or health and safety of the end users of the fabric. Be sure to do your research to uncover the nuances of each.

Other components frequently found in furniture that can be constructively selected are the springs in seats and cushions. Once again, these are elements that are hidden and easily overlooked but which can impact the sustainability quotient. If the option is available, recycled metal springs may be specified for certain pieces of furniture and would certainly be more environmentally friendly than harvesting new material to manufacture new springs. From a material perspective, steel alloys are most commonly used for manufacturing springs. Once the material is selected, the coiling process needs to happen, which can be through a cold winding or hot winding process, depending on the wire thickness. If the wire is too thick, it will need to be heated to make it malleable and easy to wind.

Once the coiling process is complete, the spring needs to be hardened, which happens through a heat treatment process in an oven. To complete the spring, the piece is taken through a series of finishing processes including grinding, if flat ends are needed on the spring; shot peening, which strengthens the steel to resist cracking and weakening throughout its lifetime; setting, to fix the targeted length and pitch of the spring; coating or electroplating, to prevent corrosion, which may also include a baking process to bind the coating; and packaging the products and material. As you can see, in this instance, it's not the actual amount of material used that's the problem. Rather, it's the repeated firing, coating, baking, and forming of springs, that requires a significant amount of energy in the manufacturing process. A primary means of saving this embodied energy is to use recycled springs in new or refurbished pieces of furniture.

The hardware used for handles, knobs, and latches is another area that merits careful consideration. These elements may be refurbished or salvaged from other furniture pieces or other applications, minimizing the use of new materials whenever possible. Otherwise, parts could be made from recycled metal or other types of materials to minimize both resources and energy consumption.

Criteria

The issue of green furniture, specifically off-gassing, is addressed in certain guidelines, although the composition of individual furniture components is not necessarily considered as part of construction projects. LEED Version 3.0 does consider furniture in its Materials and Resources section, if it is used consistently throughout a project. This is intended to allow the project team to assess whether they want to include furnishings in the credit calculations for the Materials and Resources credits. However, the team must consider the furnishings as part of the denominator, or sum of all materials that are used, in all calculations. Since the furnishings can contribute significantly to the indoor air quality of a space, many guidelines have factored them in. For example, LEED Version 3.0 for Commercial Interiors specifically includes a credit for "Low-emitting Materials—Systems Furniture and Seating" in Indoor Environmental Quality (IEQ) Credit 4.5. A number of requirements are given, such as measuring VOC emissions or being GreenGuard Indoor Air Quality Certified. There are a number of standards referenced, such as ANSI/BIFMA M7.1-2007 and ANSI/BIFMA X7.1-2007, which specifically address sustainable standards for furniture. Given this type of attention, we hope you can see how important choosing furniture with sustainable qualities can be when contributing to the greenness of a space.

Salvaged or Recycled Furniture

As with other material selections, one of the best things you can do for the environment is to use what has already been produced. Furniture that has already been manufactured would use considerably less embodied energy than furniture crafted from scratch. Even if you account for transportation, and purchase a salvaged sofa from the East Coast while you are based out West, the resources and energy saved by using an already-completed piece of furniture are substantial. And while sustainability considerations, such as toxicity or wood harvesting, may not have been taken into account when the product was first created some known problems common with newly made furniture, like off-gassing, will likely have worked themselves out by the time the furniture is repurposed. Depending on the condition of the furniture, a face-lift may be necessary.

Be sure to consider the concerns outlined earlier in this chapter and look at issues such as recycled content, off-gassing, and local sourcing. Addressing the life cycle issues of a piece of furniture, even when you are simply rehabilitating can still provide significant overall sustainability benefits.

The salvaged furniture market is still maturing. You will likely find more salvaged material (i.e. salvaged wood that you can make into a table) than actual salvaged furniture pieces in their reclaimed form. The commercial market is ahead of the residential market when it comes to salvaged office furniture, although much of the benefits of those pieces comes simply from the fact because they are being reused, not necessarily that they have any other claim to green attributes. However, like many of the other markets we've discussed thus far, it's only a matter of time before the salvaged and recycled furniture market takes off, making stock plentiful and available at a decent price point.

Resources

As with many other categories in green building, the furniture market can run amok with greenwashing. Many manufacturers and products claim that they are green, though not all have the support, testing, and research to back up those claims. Various organizations and resources have been developed to help us sift through the volumes of information and make the best choices. As always, please note that the reviews and information provided below were accurate when this book went to press, but may have changed subsequently. While the examples given below are not comprehensive, we hope we have provided enough information and insight to help you know what to start as you make your way towards sustainable furniture selections.

The primary resource for green furnishings is the Sustainable Furnishings Council (SFC; www.sustainablefurnishings. org). Formed in the fall of 2006, this nonprofit organization based in High Point, North Carolina has a Board of Directors from around the country. The council not only serves to support the selection of sustainable furnishings by buyers, but also serves as support to their members by helping them to adopt good internal practices for their companies and to act as a clearinghouse for information regarding furnishings and sustainability. The SFC mission notes that their members "take immediate steps to minimize carbon emissions, waste stream pollutants, un-recyclable content, and primary materials from unsustainable sources from any product platform under their control."

SFC's member companies are concerned with a number of sustainable issues beyond those typically found in the traditional furniture-making process. An additional—and important—issue in the members' field of vision is the incorporation of life cycle assessment issues into the product manufacturing and fabrication process. Members use the LCA framework to analyze the environmental impact of their products, providing a comprehensive and comparable baseline for consumer consideration. In line with this perspective, all wood pieces are only identified with a verifiable chain of custody, as reviewed in the previous chapter on wood. SFC members also consider and support the triple bottom line, a term that can be found repeatedly in much of the sustainability literature. While the three points of the triangle can vary by organization or definition, the basics and intentions remain the same. For example, SFC uses people/planet/profits; other organizations use economy/ecology/equity or social/environment/economic. SFC can help consumers find green manufacturers, green retailers, and green designers in the furniture industry.

The term *cradle to cradle*, discussed earlier, is also used in the world of furniture, where it was first implemented by Herman Miller. As noted in a March/April 2002 article for *green@work* magazine, "We consider [a specific Herman Miller] chair to be a very good product, one with great environmental criteria," said [a Herman Miller employee]. "But we wanted to take it apart and go entirely back through our supply chain and figure out what it took to make it, what it was made out of, and use the cradle to cradle assessment process to help us see in a much more detailed way what the performance of the chair was."[54] This quote embodies the idea behind the cradle to cradle system, which looks at the entire life cycle of products.

Chapter 11: Finishes

In this chapter, we use the general term "finishes" to refer to adhesives, sealants, coatings, and paints, largely cosmetic items that tend to start off in liquid form.

When it comes to finishes, a number of concerns emerge that pertain to the specific materials involved, how they are applied, and the potential for off-gassing from the product as it cures. At the top of the list of materials that cause concern are those that contain volatile organic compounds (VOCs), especially formaldehyde and toluene.

Formaldehyde—specifically urea formaldehyde—is considered to be harmful, highly volatile and toxic, and its use should be avoided if at all possible. Please refer back to the discussion of this in Chapters 7, 9, and 10. What was covered in these chapters applies equally as well to the use of formaldehyde in applied finishes. Toluene, the second substance we'd like to highlight, is a water-insoluble clear liquid used as a common solvent in applications such as paint thinner, or to dissolve silicone sealants. Both formaldehyde and toluene are commonly used in the traditional construction finishing process and in finishes themselves; both have been linked to harmful health effects such as nausea and impaired kidney function.

It is important to both understand and take into consideration the various application techniques for each of the finishes used in your project. Different application methods can often result in different exposure reactions for both individuals who apply the finishes and those who inhabit the space.

Aerosols present the greatest source of concern in application methods. They shrink the size of the harmful liquid or solid particles into a gaseous form, making the molecules infinitely easier to inhale and thereby increasing the possibility of lung and other internal organ exposure during the construction and application process. This would affect not only the subcontractors doing the work, but would also increase the amount of fine particles introduced into the indoor air system, thereby affecting the occupants as well.

Spray-on techniques present similar concerns, but are not considered quite as dangerous as aerosol applications because the particles are slightly bigger when they become airborne. Other application methods, such as brush on or roll on, are not of as much concern because their application can be controlled. The application concerns just described are consistent across each of the products mentioned below.

In practice, application hazards can be mediated by having subcontractors use masks and gloves, and by increasing ventilation in the immediate area to evacuate as many airborne particles as possible. Unlike other materials we have discussed, in which the sustainability concerns are related primarily to material composition, when it comes to finishes, a major consideration is the application technique that you use.

For inhabitants of the space, post-application chemical off-gassing represents one of the most significant indoor air quality concerns. While there may be very few health impacts related to the actual application of finish coats, there is the possibility for extended indoor air impacts once the substance has been applied. Paints and finishes can off-gas for many months after installation and application, becoming airborne and causing headaches, nausea, and other health effects to the occupants.

Let's look now at the most common types of finishes: adhesives, caulks and sealants, and paints and coatings.

Adhesives

While adhesives have been covered in previous chapters, such as flooring, they have many other applications that can adversely affect occupant health. Adhesives are typically found in two primary areas: gluing or laminating applications, and flooring in tiles.

The use of primers in adhesive products is the main culprit in their toxicity and negative health effects, and many manufacturers of sealants and adhesives are currently looking for ways to mitigate the amount contained in their products. Primers are a concern because of their flammability and volatility; however, any chemical transformation of the adhesive product could have an effect on how the adhesives work in to various materials. A number of traditional adhesive products contain more than 30% petroleum-derived volatile solvents that allow

> **Adhesive primers** address the porous properties of many materials that need to accept something being adhered to them. If adhesives are applied directly to porous materials, the pores will absorb the adhesive—shortening the life and minimizing the durability of the final product being adhered (i.e., carpet tiles, VCT, etc). By using an adhesive primer, usually in liquid form and made primarily of latex, the pores are filled in and the bonding abilities of the adhesives are heightened.

the product to remain in liquid form until applied.[55] These solvents are not only an exposure hazard to the installers, but will off-gas as they continue to cure, polluting the indoor air, possibly for months.

Construction materials used in the basic structural and interior components of a space, like plywood and subfloor, may contain adhesives. Carpet, linoleum, and VCT (covered in the chapter on flooring) would also be installed with adhesives. Even newer green options, such as bamboo and cork, typically use adhesives in their installation. Always be aware of the environmental impact of any adhesive you consider, and weigh your selections against the types of performance requirements needed and the durability issues for the specific installations and materials. Consider water-based, low- or zero-VOC adhesives when available and appropriate, or consider selecting materials that do not actually need adhesives and could use other fasteners such as nails, screws, or staples that can ultimately be recycled.

Caulks and Sealants

In both their makeup and application, the considerations for caulk and sealants are similar to those for adhesives. Sealants are usually used to mitigate moisture, sound, or airflow in all phases of the construction project from basic structural construction to finish applications. They enable finishes to become water resistant and/or repellant.

Fire-stopping sealants or caulks are critical to the safety of a building. When considering sustainable attributes and environmental considerations for these products, it is important to first consider the safety requirements and related building codes. The integrity and performance of sealants and adhesives that serve a safety purpose must be weighed against possible health considerations when making decisions about the most appropriate product to use. Some products may require chemicals or VOCs in order to meet the fire performance requirements. First and foremost, we ought to consider the safety of the building occupants, with indoor air quality as a secondary issue. While the two are not mutually exclusive, there are trade-offs and it is important to thoroughly understand and carefully consider the impacts of the product you are considering.

Paints and Coatings

As with many final finishes, the environmental and health considerations of paints are similar to those outlined above and in other chapters of this book. To better understand them, let's quickly review the basics of paint composition. A Johns Hopkins study suggests that there are more than 300 toxic chemicals and 150 carcinogens in traditional paints.[56] Paint has four primary ingredients: binders, pigments, solvents, and fillers, all four of which traditionally contain some synthetic components that, in turn, often contain VOCs. The binder is the primary body of the paint and holds the pigment. This can also be referred to as the "base" of the paint, which may be oil, water, or latex. The type of base chosen will depend on the surface to be painted. Alternative natural binders include chalk, animal or vegetable glues, vegetable oils, lime, flour, and milk curd. Some of the more common green replacements are clay-based wall finishes available from companies such as American Clay and Cru. Various finishes can be achieved with each type of paint, including flat, gloss, and semi-gloss. These finish choices do not generally impact the sustainability considerations of the paint itself.

Pigment is responsible for the color of the paint. While most pigments are synthetic, natural possibilities include nuts, berries, carbon, charcoal, clays, and herbs. Solvents, another primary paint ingredient, provide the paint with its liquidity and can alter the consistency of the product. They can also affect the drying time and are used for remedying mistakes in applications. Water or natural turpentine are types of solvents often used in environmentally-friendly paints. Lastly, fillers help to support the binding agent and provide texture. Chalk, talcum, and clay are frequent filler materials for paint products.

Because they are complex compounds containing an array of different materials that make up the base and pigments, paints need to be carefully reviewed for sustainable options. Paint manufacturers do not yet routinely include the source of their base materials and pigments, unless they view themselves as alternative sources and are marketing their products specifically for the alternative materials included. You will likely have to track down this information yourself through the manufacturer as it typically will not be included on the standard specification sheet.

The application of the paint—spray versus brush—affects the amount of smaller particles sent into the air. As discussed previously, an aerosol application introduces smaller particles that become airborne easily and can therefore be inhaled; for that reason alone, aerosols are the least desirable application method.

Other Finishes

In addition to sealants, adhesives, and coatings, which comprise the bulk of finishes, epoxy sealants for concrete, urethanes, stains for woods or other materials, and topcoats and other coatings also exist. Across the board, the important items to note for any interior remain the same: the number of VOCs and off-gassing of chemicals should be minimized and the least harmful application technique should be used in order to minimize the amount of particulates to which occupants could be exposed.

Selecting Paints and Finishes

It is best to choose paints made from natural raw components like water, plant oils and resins, plant dyes and oils; or minerals including chalk, clay, and bees' wax, mineral dyes, natural latex, and talcum milk casein. Most water-based natural paints emit minimal smell. Oil-based natural paints often have an enjoyable citrusy fragrance, and are typically the safest bet for both your health and the environment.[57] Also, as always, choose the lowest VOC content that will meet your needs.

Zero VOC

Paints containing VOCs below five grams/liter can be characterized as zero VOC, as outlined by the EPA Reference Test Method 24. Some paint manufacturers may declare zero VOCs, but their products may include colorants, biocides, and fungicides, each of which could contain VOCs. Simply adding a color typically brings the VOC level to near ten grams/liter, which is still low, but should be carefully considered.[57] Some more traditional paints may have VOCs that are higher still.

Low VOC

Low VOC paints, stains, and varnishes are water- instead of petroleum-based. This allows the levels of dangerous emissions to be lower than comparable solvent-borne surface coatings. Low-VOC options also contain either no, or extremely low levels of both heavy metals and formaldehyde. Though not organic compounds, these are both serious considerations for finishes. The total amount of VOCs differs among low-VOC products and adhere instead to an upper threshold. This total amount should be listed on the paint can or material datasheet.

To meet EPA standards, paints and stains cannot contain VOCs in amounts above 200 grams/liter. Varnishes have a VOC threshold of 300 grams/liter. Typically, low-VOC paints developed by highly regarded paint manufacturers meet the fifty grams/liter VOC threshold. In contrast, paints certified by the Green Seal Standard (GS-11) have lower than fifty grams/liter (for flat sheen) or 150 grams/liter (for non-flat sheen). Please note, however, that low-VOC paints will produce an odor until dry.[57, 58]

Grouts

Green considerations for grouts revolve around the chemical makeup of the material. Traditional grouts include a number of chemical additives such as epoxies and silicone, in addition to some form of aggregate, hardening agents, sealants, and dyes. Grouts can contain recycled content, such as fly ash, to reduce the embodied energy within the product. As with paints, sealants, and adhesives, VOCs in grout are often emitted while the grout dries, or cures. Some interior grouts use a damp-curing process that may take approximately three days to dry. These products are generally considered the least harmful grout treatment. Another rather obvious approach to minimizing the toxicity of grout in an interior space is to specify larger tiles, reducing the number of joints and, therefore, the amount of grout needed.

Once the interior joints have been grouted, it is likely that an additional sealant will be needed to secure them. This sealant will have its own set of considerations as outlined above.

Summary

Finishes applied inside the building space—including paints, sealants, coatings, and adhesives—can significantly affect the health of interior environments. Most of these finish materials can off-gas and introduce VOCs or other chemicals into the environment as they dry or cure. Recently, many (if not most) manufacturers have worked extensively with their internal environmental and engineering departments to introduce products that have lower VOC contents and are safer for occupant health. These healthier alternatives must be critically weighed against safety considerations that may exist for some finish and application materials so as not to compromise occupant safety. Some sealant and adhesive products require certain materials in order to adhere to fire or sound code requirements that may not meet published VOC or emission limits. Along with air quality considerations and occupant health, it is worthwhile to consider where the finishes are manufactured as well as what type of materials, natural or synthetic, are used in their composition.

Chapter 12: Future Trends

Sustainability of building materials—both as an overall consideration and an objective—continues to grow in importance, throughout the U.S. and globally. Standards and certifications that acknowledge and anoint products are maturing every day. We expect to see standardization emerge across the board for all of the materials we've included in this book; however, it's important to realize that this will not happen in one fell swoop, but rather material by material and perhaps application by application over time. In this chapter, we're pleased to describe some of the trends we see on the near horizon.

Common Credits

Over time, as different rating systems continue to assess their criteria for evaluating products, user communities will become more involved in making educated decisions about what should be amended and enhanced. We expect that convergence will begin to occur among rating systems in the acceptable criteria, causing their general intentions to become more closely aligned, even though the finer details and credit weightings will continue to be left to the discretion of the individual organizations promulgating the standards.

Ideally, as a building community, we will be able to reach agreement about what types of materials we want in our homes, offices, and other living spaces, and why. Health, safety, and productivity are common goals that are already taking hold in the credits outlined in each rating system; we expect that trend to continue to morph over time as standards are developed to accommodate more structure types, methods, and building techniques.

We hope that the array of sustainable options that are already on the market (and that we've mentioned in this book) allay the fears of some that pursuing sustainable options means compromising aesthetics. We also expect that materials providing multiple sustainable attributes will increase in popularity if for no other reason than sheer practicality: such products are more likely to contribute to multiple rating system credits, and therefore to achieving your quantitative green goals. Lastly, we expect that addressing life cycle issues will become more prominent in rating systems once some of the overarching issues with LCA are addressed, possibly through the definition of credits and credentialing, or through standards' organizations and tools.

Expansion of Attributes

The attributes that contribute to sustainability in building materials are fairly clear and agreed on by the industry:

- The product contains recycled content.
- The product is being reused in whole or in part.
- The harvesting and creation of the product is responsibly managed.
- The product is locally sourced or transportation is minimized in sourcing materials.
- The product is made from rapidly renewable source materials that have been sustainably harvested.
- The product is non-toxic.
- The product generates minimal off-gassing.
- The product is properly disposed of or recycled at the end of its useful life.

We expect that additional attributes—particularly those related to life cycle, social impacts, and the responsibility issues we discussed previously—will be increasingly incorporated into building materials. As specific LCA tools emerge, we anticipate that standards organizations will begin to include assessment criteria in their systems, ultimately making life cycle considerations a sustainable attribute that must be fulfilled to achieve any type of certification.

Consolidation of Standards

The most important feature of any certification is the integrity with which the assessment process is performed, so that the resulting information is accurate and credible. For that reason, the most useful and valuable certifications are those that entail third-party assessments of products they do not own. These independent organizations use industry-adopted criteria that are clearly defined, understood, and broadly accepted as being truly representative of the characteristics sought within the material.

As with any money-making industry, sustainability standards will proliferate (and have already done so) as a result of opportunity and demand. While some standards initiatives have been unable to gain traction and have been short-lived, others have grabbed hold firmly and are here to stay.

Some consolidation of standards has started to occur and we expect that trend to continue. We anticipate that some of the standards that arose out of opportunity, using their own assessment criteria or simply offering a label in exchange for a fee, will slowly fade away as the industry adopts more credible third-party labeling options.

Certain countries and states (California being the dominant one in the U.S.) have established stringent air quality guidelines for building materials. We expect that bodies such as the California Air Resources Board (CARB) will continue to introduce and enact testing standards that set the bar in the industry. Adoption of these standards has already begun, by building rating systems such as LEED and Green Globes, as meeting or exceeding the criteria previously established.

Growing Emphasis on LCA and Life Cycle Thinking

LCA tools, techniques, labels, and attributes are emerging; numerous task groups have formed in various organizations and have begun tackling the multitude of issues pertaining to life cycle assessment. As these efforts gain momentum, we should begin to see the next iteration of green building form and gel around some generally accepted LCA principles.

For this reason, the potential exists for LCA certifications or labels to be offered in the future, but this may take some time to come to fruition. An apple-to-apple comparison will not be feasible until an industry-wide standard for building materials is developed and accepted, in tandem with life cycle information, which can be compiled into holistic, reliable information. The need is real, however, to be able to incorporate this type of holistic thinking and labeling into products, so we hope to begin to see some early prototype labels over the next couple of years.

The formation of comprehensive databases, backed by credible, audited manufacturers' data, will help spur the pace of development and adoption of LCA tools for building materials. To be meaningful and embraced as valid, such tools require a high level of integrity in the data they use. As demand grows for such LCA tools, so too will the emphasis on reliable data.

More data will likely be provided in all material categories, so that a comprehensive comparison can be completed both between product categories and between manufacturers within specific categories. Once consolidation occurs and consensus is achieved on the leading tools, manufacturers will hurry to get their data assembled for inclusion in these databases.

As is the case with any holistic approach like this, disagreement over the ideal assessment method and general criteria is likely to continue. Numerous approaches for LCA thinking already exist (as described in Chapter 4) and these are still very much in the midst of being formed, defined, and refined. While it may be a bumpy ride for a bit, we do envision LCA of building materials will be an important and integral component of building material sustainability.

Life cycle thinking is a practice we can all engage in immediately, and the simple framework we provided at the end of Chapter 4 is intended to support and guide this type of thought process. We anticipate that customers will become more critical of building material products and the practices involved in their manufacture. You can see this criticism happening with many products currently on the market. Having a sustainability story that extends beyond just material ingredients to include harvesting, transportation, and end-of-life practices is becoming an expectation for discerning consumers. This more critical analysis of products is a trend that will stick. In light of this, many companies are adopting life cycle thinking as evidenced by the inclusion of their sustainability practices in their public documents and corporate responsibility reports.

Better Building Materials

Due to the trends occurring in enhanced standards, certifications, and labeling, the number of products on the market that engage in greenwashing techniques should decrease dramatically. Through the efforts of building materials education groups and resources like this book, the building community will become savvier in their questions and better able to ferret out the true sustainability story of any given product. Manufacturers cannot fool an educated specifier, designer, or user, especially when health and well-being are primary considerations. The days of simply using materials that claim they are green are over. Homeowners, too, have become wise to greenwashing and won't tolerate a contractor who is not diligent about making eco-conscious decisions, if that is the homeowner's mindset.

We expect not only the continuation of, but an increase in these building material micro-trends:

- the use of more locally available materials for structural components, flooring, countertops, and other interior applications;
- a growing preference for materials that incorporate more recycled content;
- increased and more refined structural and material reclamation practices as deconstruction becomes a widespread practice and profitable business;
- the introduction of new and innovative types of rapidly renewable materials to replace their longer life cycle counterparts (e.g., hardwood and natural stone);
- the elimination of petroleum-based materials, wherever possible, by building product manufacturers as well as reduced use of energy-intensive materials such as Portland cement;
- the refinement and more widespread adoption of sustainable harvesting standards, not just for trees, but also for of bio-fiber and animal-based products as well.

Large-scale changes will likely happen more slowly, but they are already well underway. Manufacturers of the heaviest and most widely used materials—concrete, steel, and drywall—have products in the pipeline that represent major technological advancements for these industries, whose histories have generally been marked by limited innovation over the past century or more. As these products emerge, not only will they change the whole equation for building materials, we are optimistic that they can make a significant improvement in the carbon footprint of the building industry for a long time to come. As consumer demand for sustainable products burgeons, can further advancements and innovation in all categories of building materials be far behind?

We anticipate that the definition, context, and expectations of sustainable features will continue to evolve, incorporating more of the issues that impact health and well-being, such as noise, ergonomics, and light, into the selection of all building materials. Furthermore, as our definitions, context, and expectations change, it is likely—perhaps even inevitable since language is a living, not static, mirror of culture—that even the terminology we use to talk about sustainability will change. Don't be surprised to see terms like "sustainable," "green," and "eco-friendly" become increasingly passé over time as consumers tire of these generic terms and find specific verbiage that is more unique and appropriate to describe green construction trends. We can easily imagine terms like "healthy-chic" and "clean building" will one day become part of the public's vernacular regarding environmentally friendly strategies. Indeed, we look forward to the day when the dual concepts of green building and sustainable living have become such universal standards, so widely implemented, that when those terms are used at all it will simply be to recall them as the forerunners of what has become the now-ubiquitous clean building and healthy-chic lifestyle.

Helpful Acronyms

Airborne Toxic Control Measure	ATCM	Collaborative for High Performance Schools	CHPS
American National Standards Institute	ANSI	Consumer Product Safety Commission	CPSC
American Society for Testing and Materials	ASTM	Consumer Product Safety Improvement Act	CPSIA
American Society of Heating, Refrigerating, and Air-Conditioning Engineers	ASHRAE	credit interpretation request	CIR
		Department of Transportation	DOT
American Tree Farm System	ATFS	di-(2-ethylhexyl) phthalate	DEHP
benzylbutyl phthalate	BzBP	diethyl phthalate	DEP
British thermal unit	BTU's	dimethyl phthalate	DMP
brominated flame retardants	BFR's	di-n-butyl phthalate	DBP
Building for Environmental and Economic Sustainability	BEE'S	Environmental Protection Agency	EPA
		environmentally preferable purchasing	EPP
Business and Institutional Furniture Manufacturer's Association	BIFMA	ethylene propylene diene monomer	EPDM
		Federal Trade Commission	FTC
California Air Resources Board	CARB	Food and Drug Administration	FDA
California's Department of Health Services	CDHS	Forestry Stewardship Council	FSC
Canadian Standards Association	CSA	Global Reporting Initiative	GRI
Carpet and Rug Institute	CRI	Green Building Initiative	GBI
chain of custody	CoC	Green Seal	GS

Greenguard Environmental Institute	GEI	No-Added Formaldehyde	NAF
Halogenated Flame Retardants	HFR's	No-Added Urea Formaldehyde	NAUF
Healthy Building Network	HBN	Occupational Safety and Health Administration	OSHA
Heating, Ventilating, and Air Conditioning	HVAC	on-center	OC
high density polyethylene	HDPE	oriented strand board	OSB
high-pressure laminate	HPL	perfluorobutane sulfonate	PFBS
Indoor Air Quality	IAQ	perfluorocarbons	PFC's
Institute for Market Transformation to Sustainability	MTS	perfluorooctanoic acid	PFOA
Insulated Concrete Forms	ICF's	persistent bioaccumulative toxics	PBT's
International Labor Organization	ILO	phenol formaldehyde	PF
International Organization for Standardization	ISO	polybrominated diphenyl ethers	PBDE
International Residential Code	IRC	polyethylene terephthalate	PET
Leadership in Energy and Environmental Design	LEED	polymeric methylene diphenyl disocyanate	pMDI
life cycle assessment	LCA	polyvinyl acetate	PVA
life cycle costing	LCC	polyvinyl chloride	PVC
life cycle impact assessment	LCIA	Program for the Endorsement of Forest Certification Systems	PEFC
life cycle inventory	LCI	
life cycle management	LCM	Resilient Floor Covering Institute	RFCI's
linear, low-density polyethylene	LLDPE	return on investment	ROI
medium-density fiberboard	MDF	Scientific Certification Systems	SCS
methylene diphenyl isocyanate	MDI	Society of Environmental Toxicology and Chemistry	SETAC
National Association of Home Builders'	NAHB	South Coast Air Quality Management District	SCAQM
National Institute of Standards and Technology	NIST	
National Renewable Energy Laboratory	NRFL	structural insulated panels	SIP's
National Sanitation Foundation	NSF	Sustainable Forestry Initiative	SFI
nitrile butadiene polymer	NBP	Sustainable Furnishings Council	SFC

The American Center for Life Cycle Assessment	ACCA
The Society of Environmental Toxicology and Chemistry	SETAC
thermoplastic polyolefin	TPO
thermoset crosslinked polyethylene	XLP
third-party certifier	TPC
Tool for the Reduction and Assessment of Chemical and Other Environmental Impacts	TRACI
U.S. Department of Energy	DOE
U.S. Green Building Council	USGBC
U.S. Public Interest Research Group	U.S. PIRG
United Nations Environment Programme	UNEP
urea formaldehyde	UF
vinyl composition tile	VCT
volatile organic compounds	VOCs

Notes

1. From Keep America Beautiful, www.kab.org

2. Environmental Protection Agency Indoor Environments Division. *Indoor Air Quality Tools for Schools: Actions to Improve IAQ.* September, 1999; www.epa.gov.

3. Environmental Protection Agency (EPA). *Indoor Air Facts No. 4 (revised): Sick Building Syndrome.* Accessed January 10, 2010 from www.epa.gov/iaq/pubs/sbs.html.

4. Fisk, William J. Address to the Harvard School of Public Health, 2000.

5. Fisk, William J. "Health and Productivity Gains from Better Indoor Environments and Their Relationship with Building Energy Efficiency." *Annual Review of Energy and the Environment,* November 25, 2000: 537–66.

6. Miller, Norm G., David Pogue, Quiana D. Gough, and Susan M. Davis. "Green Buildings and Productivity." *Journal of Sustainable Real Estate* 1.1 (2009).

7. *The Daily Green.* Accessed September 25, 2010, from www.thedailygreen.com/environmental-news/latest/phthalates-47020418#ixzz10ZCPdzOP.

8. "PVC Facts." *Healthy Building Network.* Accessed September 28, 2010, from www.healthybuilding.net/pvc/facts.html.

9. The Association of Post-consumer Plastic Recyclers. *APR Takes A Stand on PVC* (press release). Washington, DC: April 14, 1998.

10. *Assessment of a Technical Basis for a PVC-Related Materials Credit in LEED.* Washington, D.C.: U.S. Green Building Conference, February, 2007.

11. Environmental Protection Agency (EPA). *Sources of Indoor Air Pollution: Formaldehyde.* Accessed September 28, 2010, from www.epa.gov/iaq/formalde.html.

12. From the Healthy Building Network, www.healthybuilding.net/formaldehyde/.

13. *PSI Green Expectations.* Accessed September 28, 2010, from www.panelsource.net/resourcecenter/greenbulletins.

14. Environmental Protection Agency (EPA). *An Introduction to Indoor Air Quality, Organic Gases (Volatile Organic Compounds).* Accessed September 28, 2010, from http://www.epa.gov/iaq/voc.html.

15. Lenssen, Nicholas and David Malin Roodman. "Worldwatch Paper 124, A Building Revolution: How Ecology and Health Concerns are Transforming Construction." *Worldwatch Institute* (1995).

16. U.S. Department of Energy, Energy Information Administration. *Assumptions to the Annual Energy Outlook,* 2008.

17. U.S. Department of Energy, Environmental Information Administration. *EIA Annual Energy Outlook,* 2008.

18. U.S. Department of Energy, Environmental Information Administration. *EIA Annual Energy Outlook,* 2008.

19. U.S. Geological Survey, 2000.

20. U.S. Environmental Protection Agency. *Estimating 2003 Building-Related Construction and Demolition Materials Amounts,* 2009.

21. Environmental Protection Agency (EPA). *Characterization of Municipal Solid Waste in the United States.* Report No. EPA 530/R-98-007, 1997.

22. Adapted from The Zero Waste Alliance, www.zerowaste.org.

23. McDonough, William, and Michael Braungart. *Cradle to Cradle: Remaking the Way We Make Things.* San Francisco, CA: North Point Press, 2002.

24. MBDC Cradle to Cradle Certification, www.c2ccertified.com/.

25. The Forest Stewardship Council (FSC), www.fscus.org/.

26. International Labor Rights Forum, www.laborrights.orgabout-ilrf.

27. Bureau of Labor Statistics, November, 2009, www.bls.gov/iif/.

28. Fair Trade Federation, www.fairtradefederation.org.

29. Savitz, Andrew W. and Karl Weber. *The Triple Bottom Line: How Today's Best-Run Companies Are Achieving Economic, Social, and Environmental Success—and How You Can Too.* San Francisco, CA: Jossey-Bass, 2006.

30. The Global Reporting Initiative, www.globalreporting.org.

31. *Greenguard.* Accessed January 17, 2010, from www.greenguard.org/pricing.

32. International Organization for Standardization (ISO). *Environmental Management, Life-Cycle Assessment, Principles and Framework.* International Standard 14040, 2006.

33. Environmental Protection Agency, Office of Research and Development. *Life Cycle Assessment: Inventory Guidelines and Principles,* EPA/600/R-92/245, February, 1993.

34. Environmental Protection Agency. *Tool for the Reduction and Assessment of Chemical and Other Environmental Impacts (TRACI): User's Guide and System Documentation,* EPA/600/R-02/052. Cincinnati, OH: EPA Office of Research and Development, August 2002.

35. Steen, B. *A Systematic Approach to Environmental Priority Strategies in Product Development (EPS).* Version 2000, CPM Report 1999: 4 and 5. Chalmers University, Göteborg, 1999.

36. Frischknecht, R. et. al. *Swiss Ecological Scarcity Method: The New Version 2006.* Berne, Switzerland, 2006.

37. Goedkoop, M. and R. Spriensma. *The Eco-Indicator '99: A Damage Oriented Method for Life Cycle Impact Assessment.* VROM Zoetermeer, Nr. 1999/36A/B, 2nd edition. April, 2000.

38. International Organization for Standardization (ISO). *Environmental Management, Life-Cycle Assessment, Principles and Framework.* International Standard 14040, 2006.

39. ASTM International. *Standard Practice for Measuring Life-Cycle Costs of Buildings and Building Systems.* ASTM Designation E917-05, West Conshohocken, PA, 2005.

40. ASTM International. *Standard Practice for Applying the Analytic Hierarchy Process to Multiattribute Decision Analysis of Investments Related to Buildings and Building Systems.* ASTM Designation E1765-02, West Conshohocken, PA, 2002.

41. ASTM International. *Standard Classification for Building Elements and Related Sitework—UNIFORMAT II*. ASTM Designation E1557-05, West Conshohocken, PA, 2005.

42. From www.greenerbuildings.com/news/2007/02/13/leed-include-buildings-lifecycle-evaluations.

43. Athena Institute Eco Calculator, www.athenasmi.org/tools/ecoCalculator/index.html.

44. U.S. Life Cycle Inventory Database, www.nrel.gov/lci.

45. More information on this topic can be found at www.ecotimber.com/guide/flooring-sustainability-health.html.

46. From www.dreamfox.com.cn/english/research_by_experts_and_leaders_detail.asp?id=22).

47. From www.immune.com/rubber/nr1.html.

48. Farrelly, David. The Book of Bamboo. San Francisco, CA: Sierra Club Books, 1984.

49. Adams, Mike. "Indoor Air in Homes Often Contaminated with Formaldehyde from Building Materials." *Natural News.com.* Accessed July 28, 2010, from www.naturalnews.com/023202_formaldehyde_health_homes.html.

50. From www.arb.ca.gov/toxics/compwood/compwood.htm.

51. From www.cpsc.gov.

52. From www.cpsc.gov.

53. From www.vpirg.org/node/98; www.uspirg.org/uspirg.asp?id2=19703; www.ewg.org/node/17939.

54. Accessed November 24, 2009, from www.greenatworkmag.com/gwsubaccess/02marapr/eco.html.

55. Accessed December 21, 2009 from www.ecoact.org/Programs/Green_Building/green_Materials/adhesives.htm.

56. Dadd, Debra L. *Home Safe Home.* New York, NY: Tarcher, 1997.

57. From www.eartheasy.com.

58. As with all standards, these are current at the time of publication. Please be sure to do your own research as you specify products for your projects.

Index

Note: Italicized page locators indicate a figure.

anti-static treatments, carpet products and, 122
appliances, with Energy Star logo, 69
ARCAT, 74
architects, indoor air quality and, 39
asbestosis, 134
ASHRAE. *see* American Society of Heating, Refrigerating, and Air-Conditioning Engineers (ASHRAE)
ash wood flooring, 111
Asia, natural stone countertop material from, 132
Association of Post-consumer Plastics Recyclers, 33
ATCM. *see* Airborne Toxic Control Measure (ATCM)
ATFS. *see* American Tree Farm System (ATFS)
Athena Institute, 83
    databases maintained by, 87
    EcoCalculator for Assemblies, 86, 87, 89
    Impact Estimator for Buildings, 82, 86, 87
Avonite
    countertops, 127
    plastic-based solid surfacing, 131

B

bamboo, 144, 147
    adhesives and installation of, 157
    in butcher block countertops, 137
    for millwork, 140–41
    NAHB renewable materials section and, 23
    as rapidly renewable material, 50
bamboo flooring, 112, 115–16
    alternatives/best choices for, 116
    composition of, 115
    concerns and objections about, 116
    cost of, wood floors *vs.*, 26
    trends and evolution of, 116–17
barns, reclaimed boards from, 144
base material, for engineered flooring, 114
bathrooms, countertops in, 127
batts, 102
    blue cotton, 104
    of insulation, 102

B-Corporations, 55, 56
beech wood, salvaged, 113
BEES. *see* Building for Environmental and Economic Sustainability (BEES)
bees' wax, paints made from, 159
benzylbutyl phthalate (BzBP), 31, 166
berries, in paint pigments, 158
Beyond Formaldehyde, 36
BFRs. *see* brominated flame retardants (BFRs)
BIFMA. *see* Business and Institutional Furniture Manufacturer's Association (BIFMA)
binders
    natural, 158
    in paints, 157–58
bioaccumulative toxic chemicals, reducing release of, 40
bio-based boards, as rapidly renewable material, 50
bio-based carpet fibers, 122
biodiversity, cork harvesting and, 117, 118
biosphere, cork forests and, 117
birch wood, salvaged, 113
Bis (2-ethyl-hexyl phthalate), 31
bitumen, modified, for roof membranes, 40
B Lab, 55, 56
black walnut, salvaged, 113
blankets, of insulation, 102
"bloom effect," with linoleum, 121
blue cotton batts, 104
borates, recycled denim insulation soaked in, 104
branding, life cycle thinking and, 91–92
Braungart, Michael, 44
Brazilian cherry wood flooring, 111
British thermal units (BTUs), 166
brominated flame retardants (BFRs), 32, 40, 166
brownfield development, NAHB, site selection and, 21
BTUs. *see* British thermal units (BTUs)
Building and Institutional Furniture Manufacturer's Association (FIFMA), 166

building envelope, sealing, chemical effects related to, 23
Building for Environmental and Economic Sustainability (BEES), 83, 86, 87–88, 166
building materials selection. *see* materials selection
building products, SMART certification for, 71
building reuse
    LEED and, 21
    life cycle discussion and, 20–21
    NAHB's standards and, 21
buildings
    deconstruction of, 112
    Energy Star qualified, 69
built environment, impact of, on natural environment, 42
Bureau of Labor Statistics, 53
business, life cycle thinking in, 91–82
Business and Institutional Furniture Manufacturer's Association (BIFMA), Furniture Sustainability Standard, 148–49
business furniture
    environmental impact and, 149–49
    intelligent design and, 149
butcher block countertops, 136–37
    concerns and objections about, 137
    wood used in, 136–37
buy-back programs, furniture and, 149
byproduct fibers, for millwork, 141
BzBP. *see* benzylbutyl phthalate (BzBP)

C

cabinetry, built-in, 138
cabling, 99
calcining, of gypsum, 106
California Air Resources Board (CARB), 36, 62, 144, 163, 166
California Indoor Air Quality Specifications, for Open Panel Office Furniture, 61–62
California's Department of Health Service (CDHS), 166